Development in Developing Economies

About the Editors

Mihir Kumar Pal is a Associate Professor and former Head of the Department of Economics at the Vidyasagar University, Midnapore, West Bengal, India. He stood First in the First Class in both BA(Hons.) and MA(Economics) and was awarded Gold Medals. He obtained M.Phil(Economics) from University of Calcutta and Ph.D. (Economics) from Kalyani University. He has published several articles in reputed national and international journals. He has also presented papers in national and international conferences. Other published books of Dr. Pal are *Productivity in the Organised Manufacturing Sector in India* (*Concept, and Development Alternatives—Theories and Evidence* (Allied).

Sebak Kumar Jana is currently Reader at the Department of Economics with Rural Development, Vidyasagar University in West Bengal. Dr. Jana after graduating from Presidency College, Kolkata obtained M.Sc. degree in Economics from University of Calcutta, and then obtained M.Phil. and Ph.D. in Economics from Jadavpur University, Kolkata. His area of research includes environmental economics, energy economics, agricultural economics and economics of education. He has published articles in both national and international journals. He is also associated with national and international projects.

Development in Developing Economies

Edited by

Mihir Kumar Pal
Sebak Kumar Jana

CONCEPT PUBLISHING COMPANY PVT. LTD.
NEW DELHI-110059

ISBN-13 : 978-81-8069-840-8

First Published 2012

Published and Printed by

Concept
Since 1974

Concept Publishing Company Pvt. Ltd.
A/15-16, Commercial Block, Mohan Garden
New Delhi-110059 (India)
T: 25351460, 25351794, *F*: 091-11-25357109
E: publishing@conceptpub.com, W: www.conceptpub.com
Editorial Office: H-13, Bali Nagar, New Delhi-110 015, India.

Cataloging in Publication Data--*Courtesy:* D.K. Agencies (P) Ltd. <docinfo@dkagencies.com>

Development in developing economies / edited by Mihir Kumar Pal, Sebak Kumar Jana.
p. cm.
Includes bibliographical references and index.
ISBN 9788180698408

1. Economic development—India—Congresses. 2. Economic development—Developing countries—Congresses. 3. India—Economic conditions—Congresses. 4. Developing countries—Economic conditions—Congresses. 5. Industrialization—India—Congresses. 6. Industrialization—Developing countries—Congresses. 7. India—Economic policy—Congresses. 8. Developing countries—Economic policy—Congresses. I. Pal, Mihir Kumar, 1965- II. Jana, Sebak Kumar.

DDC 338.954 23

Preface

Issues of development are the most important agenda for the present day society. The issues differ from region to region and country to country. Obviously the issues of development also differ from developed to developing countries. A good number of issues are throwing up enormous challenges in the paths of development of developing countries. In this backdrop the Department of Economics with Rural Development, Vidyasagar University, Midnapore, West Bengal had organized a National Seminar on "Issues of Development in Developing Economies". The present book is an outcome of this seminar. The book consists of ten selected papers presented in the seminar. The papers highlight some contemporary issues in developing economies like development theories, globalization and liberalization, industrial development, agricultural development, environmental economics and insurance sector development. The present volume aims at presenting some conceptual, theoretical and empirical issues to understand the contemporary development problems.

We convey our heartfelt thanks to all the contributors of the book. We are also indebted to the faculty members of our Department for giving their valuable suggestions. Thanks are also due to the referees of the papers for their comments according to which the papers have been revised.

We would also like to express our gratitude to the University Grants Commission for the financial support in organizing the seminar and in publishing the book.

Last but not the least we are immensely indebted to the Concept Publishing Company Pvt. Ltd. New Delhi for publishing the book.

Contents

List of Contributors

Dr. Hirendra Nath Roy, Former Professor, Department of Economics, University of Calcutta, Kolkata, West Bengal, India.

Dr. Raj Kumar Sen, Professor, Department of Economics, Rabindra Bharati University, Kolkata, West Bengal.

Dr. Jayanta Sen, Assistant Professor, West Bengal State University, Barasat, Kolkata, West Bengal, India.

Dr. Anindita Basu (Chowdhury), Lecturer, Department of Economics, Mahishadal Raj College, Mahishadal, Midnapur(East), West Bengal, India.

Sarbapriya Ray, Senior Lecturer, Deptt. of Commerce, Shyampur Siddheswari Mahavidyalaya, Howrah, West Bengal.

Dr. Mihir Kumar Pal, Associate Professor, Deptt. of Economics, Vidyasagar University, Paschim Medinipur, West Bengal.

Dr. Sebak Kumar Jana, Reader, Deptt. of Economics with Rural Development, Vidyasagar University, Paschim Medinipur, West Bengal.

Mr. Debasish Barik, Research Scholar, Department of Economics with Rural Development, Vidyasagar University, Paschim Medinipur, West Bengal.

Arghya Kusum Mukharjee, Lecturer in Economics, Srikrishna College, Nadia, West Bengal.

Dr. Amit Kundu, Reader, Department of Economics, Jadavpur University, Kolkata, West Bengal, India.

Dr. Arabinda Ghosh, Reader, Department of Economics, Raghunathpur College, Raghunathpur, Purulia, West Bengal, India.

Dr. Subrata Kundu, Department of Economics, Vivekananda Satavarshiki Mahavidyalaya, Manikpara, Paschim Medinipur, West Bengal, India.

Dr. Joy Chakraborty, Lecturer of Finance & Accounts, NSHM Business School, Kolkata, West Bengal, India.

Introduction

Issues of development are the most important agenda for the present day society. The issues differ from region to region and country to country. Obviously the issues of development also differ from developed to developing countries. A good number of issues are throwing up enormous challenges presently in the paths to development of developing countries. In this backdrop the Department of Economics with Rural Development, Vidyasagar University, Midnapore, West Bengal had organized a National Seminar on "*Issues of Development in Developing Economies*". The present book is an outcome of this seminar. The book consists of ten papers presented in the seminar. The papers highlight some contemporary issues in developing economies. The broad issues covered in this volume include some key issues in developing economies like thoughts on development theories, globalization, liberalization, industrial development, agricultural development, environment and insurance.

The first chapter containing the paper entitled "Some Thoughts on Development Economics" has been written by Hirendranath Roy. The paper traces thoughts on economic development in the context of backward economies. He discusses critically about the theories put forward by Adam Smith, Marshall, Nurkse, Ricardo, Ranis and Fie, Pigou, Tinbergen, Chenery, Keynes, Harrod, Domar, Solow, Tobin, Rosenstein — Rodan, Kaldor, Hirschman, Amartya Sen etc. According to him, the main points thrown up by development literature are as follows. In the first place, we need to synthesize alternative paradigms so that we can understand the operation of the forces promoting or hindering economic development. Secondly, in order to effectuate this synthesis economist will have to judge the relevance of these paradigms against the historical experience of developing countries. Lastly, economists should identify unresolved and newly emerging issues in development economics and chalk out lines of enquiry for their resolution. In recent years when the various LDCs have been adopting economic reforms of varying intensity and are feeling the impact of globalization new challenges are cropping up. They must be faced boldly and tackled efficiently.

The paper of Raj Kumar Sen (Chapter 2) deals with broad overview of some disquieting issues of development in developing countries. In his paper he has tried to identify and analyze these issues both from national and global perspectives including their regional dimensions in some cases. The most important disquieting issue of development according to many is the fall-out of the ongoing economic reforms-based development paradigm after two decades and the urgent need to reform the reform process. He has analysed the problem of the jobless growth through corporate-led industrialization under globalization resulting into disempowerment of the masses. The other is the utter neglect of agriculture and adoption of unsustainable policies affecting negatively both the poor and also the environment. With these is also associated the problem of rapidly increasing inequalities in income and wealth with the derogatory consequences on every aspect of life and culture of the present and future generations. The issue of the lack of good governance is also closely associated with this process though it existed from the ancient times. He has also discussed the other global issue affecting a large number of developing countries is that of global warming leading to adverse climate changes going to be very serious in the not so distant future. According to him a holistic and political economy approach may help us to proceed to the right direction.

Globalization started around 1980s and became widespread and more pronounced in the world economy in the 1990s. Several countries have removed restrictions on trade, movement of capital and finance and transfer of technology in order to integrate the domestic economy with the global economy. In Chapter 3 Jayanta Sen deals with the issue of globalization and poverty in the context of SAARC countries. An attempt has been made in this paper to identify the impact of globalisation on incidence of poverty in the SAARC countries. Nature and extent of globalization and its relationship with poverty is analytically discussed.

The paper by Anindita Basu in Chapter 4 analyzes the impact of trade liberalization through foreign capital inflow on the incidence of child labour and on the level of welfare of a developing economy in the Harris-Todaro (1970) framework with agricultural dualism and foreign enclave. This paper shows that under some reasonable conditions this foreign capital inflow reduces the incidence of child labour and it may improve the national welfare. The present paper also shows that the level of urban unemployment increases due to inflow of foreign capital. The analysis thus shows a trade off between increase in welfare and increase in urban unemployment as a result of foreign capital inflow in the presence of agricultural dualism.

In Chapter 5 Sarbapriya Ray and Mihir Kumar Pal seeks to measure performance of Indian Iron and Steel Industry in the light of capacity utilization and tries to assess the impact of liberalization on capacity utilization of the said Industry. The paper points out that capacity utilization has not improved after the path-breaking economic reforms in 1991 and liberalization has its significant negative impact on capacity utilization during post-reform period. This paper also deals with various issues like competition etc. being faced by Indian Iron and Steel Industry in the post-liberalized scenario. Using Porter model, they conclude that overall competition in Iron and Steel Industry has been increased during the post-reform period. Ijiri-Simon method for evaluating degree of competition reveals that nearly half of the firms in the industry have shown a declining trend in internal competition. Some major demerits of liberalization have also been discussed. There is an urgent need for developing a comprehensive plan for Iron and Steel Industry in India so that it can survive in the post-liberalized Indian environment and make its presence global.

The Pulp and Paper Industry is one of the major polluting industries in India. It is very pertinent to investigate which factors largely explain the environmental perforamance of the industry. The paper by Sebak Kumar Jana and Debasish Barik in Chapter 6 is based on the primary survey data collected from sixteen paper mills in the states of Uttar Pradesh and West Bengal in India. The paper reveals that there is a close link between environmental performance and economic efficiency of the plants among other factors.

Access to credit might be an efficient way of reducing poverty, particularly during the credit market failure. This paper of Mukherjee and Kundu in Chapter 7 tries to investigate two basic questions: (a) What are the determinants of SGSY participation and (b) How much effective the programme has been in targeting the desired beneficiaries? The District of Murshidabad, West Bengal, has been chosen as the field of study. All the selected SHG members were two years old. The initial sampling was done in 2006 to know about the socio-economic conditions of the prospective participants before joining the group. The paper finds that with the increase of education and wealth initially the likelihood of joining the SGSY increases, but after a certain level of education and wealth the probability of participating SGSY declines. It is evaluated that the programme has not been successful in achieving its avowed goals and suffers from both Type-I and Type-II errors.

In view of the critical state of the farming community in India agricultural insurance has recently been considered as an important mechanism to address the risk associated with farm output and income. The paper of Arabinda Ghosh in Chapter 8 deals with the agricultural insurance in India. Since the introduction of National Agricultural Insurance Scheme (NAIS) from 'rabi' of 1999-2000 almost a decade has passed without making much headway in mitigating our farmers' plight. Compulsory coverage of loanee farmers and even very low premium rates are not proved sufficient to cover not more than twenty per cent of the nation's farmers. Lack of access to institutional loans, failure to design suitable insurance product, inability to provide effective coverage of farmers, delay in settling claims and a very high claim-premium ratio hinder the success of the scheme. The performance of NAIS has been studied in some districts of West Bengal. The preliminary study reveals the policy goals and objectives of the scheme seem far from achievable. Yet a decade's experience could help for suitable modification of the scheme for progress of the farm sector in the end.

The study of Subrata Kundu in Chapter 9 attempts to estimate the decomposition of output growth into input growth, technology growth and change in technical efficiency of West Bengal agriculture using district level input-output data for a period of about twenty years. The entire period under study is divided into two as pre- and post-macro reform periods, i.e., 1980-89 and 1990-2000, respectively. The non-parametric DEA approach is used to estimate the results. It has been seen that throughout the period West Bengal agriculture experienced low rate of technological progress together with gradual improvements in technical efficiency but output growth in the sector becoming increasingly dependendent on input growth.

The Life Insurance sector in India has witnessed a revolutionary change since it was privatized in 1999. The privatization of the country's insurance sector saw the emergence of private and foreign players at the scene. Further, the presence of the global insurance giants has brought new innovative products, smart marketing concepts apart from the aggressive selling and distribution strategies. The market share of the private players has also increased significantly since post-liberalization. The paper by Joy Chakraborty in Chapter 10 unveils the pros and cons associated with the development of the country's one of the most emerging sectors and the efforts that are undertaken to sustain its growth momentum.

Vidyasagar University
Midnapore

Mihir Kumar Pal
Sebak Kumar Jana

1
Development Economics

Hirendra Nath Roy

Development economics, as a sub-branch of economics, emerged as a special discipline only after the Second World War. In the initial phase, there were certain factors that governed the nature and direction of research. These factors may be classified into three groups. First, there was a new urgency and concern among many nations as to how quickly we can develop the economy. Secondly, an incentive was provided for empirical research by the inter-war and war-time experiences. Economists gained valuable knowledge from such researches which formed the foundation for theorizing and construction of policy-oriented models. Finally, there was a realization among the economists that certain tools which were already available could be used to create analytical constructs. There was a belief that these constructs would deepen our understanding of the process of economic development and the role of the state in expediting growth.

Even a glance at the history of economic thought reveals that much earlier than the Second World War period there were enough discussions about "economic backwardness" which, of course, is the obverse side of the development coins. In fact even Adam Smith in his *Wealth of Nations* was, in a way, concerned with this problem. In that *magnum opus*, he searched for the nature and causes, of the growth of wealth of an economy. This means that, at the back of his mind, there lurked the basic question of economics: why a country is undeveloped and economically backward? Smith's analysis of backwardness was quite old-fashioned. He did not have suitable analytical tools for this purpose. Truly speaking, he was not a development theorist in the sense in which we use the term today. His ideas, though relevant for development, could not be integrated into an inter-temporal model which captures the essential features of LDCs. That is why Smith's analysis did not have direct impact on development theories of recent vintage. Coming to more recent times we find that those who contributed most in this area are social anthropologists, intellectually bent colonial administrators and, especially, nationalist economic thinkers in countries such as India. The colonial administrators and social anthropologists pointed out that institutional arrangements in backward countries were unsuitable for initiating growth. In these discussions, there is hardly any mention of economic problems. Nationalist thinkers in India drew inspiration from Friedrick List of Germany and thought that 'protection' from foreign competition would solve our problem for them, development was primarily a matter of pursuing appropriate policy by the Government. M.G. Ranade emphatically stated that a foreign colonial government. would never adopt such policies beneficial for the country.[1]

From early 1950s and thereafter technical economists seriously faced the problem of economic backwardness and searched for its solution. In 1965 John Boeke wrote an interesting essay where he said that economic calculations of the Western type were inapplicable in Eastern countries. The reason he advanced is that colonial dominance in these countries led to the emergence of a dual economy consisting of two sectors—one small advanced modern sector, which grew as an isolated enclave, and the other the backward traditional sector. Between these two sectors there were hardly any linkage.[2] This concept of dual economy plays an important part in the construction of development theory. Curiously enough, even Alfred Marshall, the noted British neo-classical economist, whose interests lied elsewhere, had some positive view about how backward developing countries could prosper. His views are scattered throughout his *principles*.[3] He thought in order to understand the complexity of backwardness very limited number of analytical tools were necessary. If attitudes towards work and thrift of the people could be altered then development process would start. In his opinion, these could be altered through continued exposure to the influence exerted by the advanced countries especially through trade. Anyone acquainted with economics history of our country knows that this Marshallian prediction has been proved to be empirically false. Trade became an instrument of exploitation rather than that of growth.

In India a change in perspective took place especially after we achieved independence. The faith in neo-classical economics was gone. There are definite reasons for this. Empirical experience falsified predicted neo-classical outcomes. But the loss of faith was essentially due to the impact of Keynesian economics. As a result, development economists jettisoned the central assumption of neo-classical theorizing that markets always clear at an appropriate set of prices. Keynes showed that this does not happen. This is all at the theoretical plane. Empirical experiences during the inter-war period, as I have mentioned, also had played a part. For some time Ragnor Nurkse's book '*Problems of Capital Formation in Underdeveloped Countries*'[4] becomes a Bible for students of development economics. Formerly, the idea was that it was capital shortage that acted as a bottleneck in developing countries. But the presence of massive rural under-employment meant that the capital constraint was not invariably a binding force. There was a potential source of capital in rural areas that could be utilized by appropriate policy. Earlier Michael Kalicki, in a review of Mikhail Monoilesco's book expressed the same opinion.[5] He argued that the assumption of a given supply of capital is not universally acceptable. The supply of new savings in an agricultural country was by no means fixed since unemployment, open or disguised, might be utilized for creating additional savings. In almost Keynesian fashion he added that "the new savings will be undertaken, (whose upper limit is that at which full employment is reached,) and this will continue till full employment is reached." Kalecki's seminal ideas expressed here later became a cornerstone of development economics by the 1950s.

By now it is evident from what I have said that the economists who dealt with developmental problems admitted that economic calculus had its role. But at the same time structural specificities of LDCs need to be taken into account. The belief that there is infinite elasticity of labour supply generated skepticism about the so-called 'scarcity' view of economics. During the early fifties of the last century a debate went on as to whether 'Growth' *versus* 'Choice' dichotomy was a more appropriate approach. Neo-classical economics was considered largely incapable of answering questions relating to development of Third World Countries. This is because it lacked the insights provided by subsequent analytical advances in dealing with imperfect and asymmetric information as well as absence of contingent markets. Being dissatisfied with neo-classical paradigm the development theorists turned to classical writers for enlightenment. Arthur Lewis, the Nobel Laureate, was the most prominent among them. In an influential article of 1954[6], Lewis, like Ricardo and Marx, argued that profit was the main source of savings and the supply of labour was infinitely elastic at some real wage rate. This infinite elasticity is due to the operation of Malthusian factors in Ricardo, and to the reserve army of unemployed (sustained through endogenous technical progress) in Marx. In Lewis, it is the existence of large scale unemployment and disguised unemployment that ensures 'unlimited' supply of labour to capitalist enterprises. It is also assumed that the extended joint family system or feudal practices in the subsistence sector make wages conform to average rather than marginal productivity of labour, which for overpopulated countries like India and China is perceived to be close to zero. Lewis wrote another article in 1958 entitled 'Unlimited Labour: Further Notes'[7], where he reiterated his earlier view. Sukhomoy Chakravarty in an article[8] rightly commented that Lewis model is a hybrid one. It consists of both classical and neo-classical features, which, in his words, restored a modified neo-classical mode of reasoning to a position of primacy.

The Lewis type dual economy model has been modified and extended to analyse the role of agriculture in the process of development. Retaining the major elements of the Lewis framework some economists like Ranis and Fei[9], Avinas Dixit[10] and others trace the time profile of the economy. When supply of food to the non-agricultural sector is not perfectly elastic, terms of trade are endogenous and investment in both agriculture and industry responds positively to their respective rate of profit. In this context a movement in the terms of trade against industries gives a boost to agricultural investment and thereby helps to prevent a slowdown in industrial growth. This outcome, however, depends upon some crucial conditions. Investment in agriculture has to be land-augmenting and overall factor productivity must improve. Then again agriculture has to be modernized or capitalistic and there should be no impediments to the operation of the market mechanism. These conditions are not met automatically and definite policies need to be adopted.

In development literature there has been a refrain that market mechanism does not work in low-income countries. There are two important empirical issues that plague the low income countries: (a) existence of a large reserve army of labour, and (b) low elasticity of demand and supply in important areas like foreign trade. In view of these, solution of the problem of low-level stagnation cannot come through the operation of market mechanism. In other words, the LDCs suffer from what is called 'market failure'. This perception led some economists to advocate for planning as a method for curing the malady of backwardness. The market-failure argument was first broached by Pigou in his famous book: *The Economics of Welfare*.[11] The Pigovian argument was strengthened by economists like Rosenstein-Rodan[12] and Scitovsky[13] who reinterpreted the concept of 'externalities' in a way which was much more critical of the market mechanism than what Pigou thought. Between the two Scitovsky was more perceptive. His argument is regarded as variant of modern argument of 'missing market', especially in regard to the futures markets, which neo-classical theory considers to be essential to sustain the argument that competitive equilibrium over time is, in some sense, an optimal one.[14]

Meanwhile due to the initiative of Raul Prebisch[15] working for ECLA the theory of development programming was formulated. Prebisch questioned the mutual profitability of the international division of labour for developing countries on existing lines. He looked at the relation between trade and development from the standpoint of the balance of payments rather than real resources. He argued that the unfavourable impact of unrestricted trade on the terms of trade and balance of payments of LDCs far outweighed any advantage with respect to a more efficient allocation of resources. His concern was with two distinct, but not unrelated, phenomena. One is the transference of benefits of technical progress from the less developed to the developed countries. The second is the balance of payments effect of differences in the income elasticity of demand for different types of products. He divided the world into industrial 'centres' and 'peripheral' countries and then carried his analysis within the framework of the traditional two-country, two-commodity case of international trade theory—equating the less developed countries with primary producers (the 'periphery') and the developed countries secondary producers (the 'Centre').

In the area of development programming Jan Tinbergen's contribution is noteworthy.[16] Soviet experience of planning influenced Indian planners at the time when second five-year plan was formulated. Mahalonobis[17] played a leading part in Indian discussion. His approach, however, was a structuralist, rather than a Marxist one. The characteristics of Mahalonobis's two-sector and four-sector models are well known, and I avoid any detailed analysis of them. Only comment which I like to make is that his models reflected an unbalanced growth path in view of given initial conditions and non-shiftable capital stock.

Now I turn to what is known as 'two-gap' or 'dual-gap' model. This is developed in the context of an open economy. The proponents on this model are Chenery and Bouno.[18] It is argued that there are two gaps that plague any open developing economy. One is the trade gap and the other is the savings gap. If the export-import is dominant and foreign exchange is scarce, domestic resource may remain unutilized in the absence of development policies to equate the trade gap and the savings-investment gap *ex anti*. Potential saving will decline either through a fall in the potential level of output or through a fall in the propensity to save through a redirection of expenditure. One obvious policy, however, is to devote more domestic resources to import substitution or export promotion. The two-gap has been criticized. The assumption that inadequate foreign exchange may act as an independent bottleneck is highly questionable. In fact some critics think that the initial formulations of the model were not fully specified. The experiences of Latin American countries tell us a different story. These countries had been suffering from acute inflationary hardships. Their inflation was what is called structural inflation. Theoretical model of structural inflation was developed. In structural inflation model the growth of money supply is seen to be endogenously determined by budget deficits. Governments are placed in a compulsive situation and are forced to have recourse to budget deficits because there are internal distributional struggles which are usually aggravated by the terms of trade loss. This is quite a common experience of many developing countries, including India.

Did Keynes say anything positive pertaining to the problem of economic development? The answer is yes, but not directly relating to the problems of underdeveloped countries. In 1933 Keynes wrote an article entitled "*Economic Possibilities for Our Grandchildern*"[19], where he perhaps dealt with a simple type of growth model. In this essay, we can find a use of what we understand by the concept of 'capital-output ratio'. But this, however, does not mean that here Keynes was concerned with the problem of 'underdevelopment' in the modern sense of the term. Keynes developed the idea 'land trap' as a possible explanation for arrested growth in certain phases of history in some countries. He thought the excessive preference for "gold", historically described since the days of Pliny, as one reason why Indians could not develop the productive potential of their country. It must be noted that these comments, though pertinent, do not fundamentally affect the basic logical structure of his argument of *General Theory*. One point needs to be emphasised. Keynes was thinking that, irrespective of the nature of market imperfections, the market mechanism was unable to achieve full utilization of productive potential of an economy. Keynes here was not giving us a simple theory of 'duo-economics', as some critics think. He was indeed asserting that institutions do significantly matter in determining final outcomes. In support of this view we can point to the nature of the bargaining process in the labour market. This is a major social institution which equilibrium theory in its conventional formulation cannot adequately handle. But Keynes never thought that there were different economic theories, one for 'fully employed economy' and the other for an 'underemployed economy'. Hicksian view that Keynes's 'General theory' was not a 'general theory' but just 'depression economics' is not right. Keynes's pamphlet 'How to pay for the war' is a standing refutation of this view. In three major ways Keynes influenced the formulation of development economics: (a) by devising a methodology of duelling with economic aggregate, for which empirical correlates could be estimated, (b) by questioning the alleged optimal characteristics of market economies, and (c) by showing the necessity and effectiveness of public intervention in managing the economic system.

Finally, Keynes realized that the need for a 'new international order' by setting up or helping to set up institutions, which will lead to a more broad-based global development process. He believed that restoration of *laissez faire* could not solve the complex problems arising out of the war. Thus, Keynes played a decisive role to bring about a change in the climate of opinion. This might have helped in creating some sort of a 'development consensuses' among economists of Keynesian persuasion who did much to promote it.

On the basis of Keynes's thinking in the General Theory, both Harrod[20] and Domar[21] constructed a growth model. They worked independently, but there were similarities in there constructs. They indicated two factors which could contribute to growth: (1) the aggregate investment ratio, and/or (2) the incremental capital-output ratio. Harrod-Domar model influenced development economists. They identified three major routes through which LDCs could secure rapid growth in the overall productivity of capital. First, after allowing for indivisibilities and increasing returns, the allocation of investment should be such that there are no serious sectoral/bottlenecks or excess capacity. Secondly, given the initial structural imbalance and the wide disparity in the productivity of capital and labour across various lines of economic activity. Capital accumulation needs to be faster in those sectors where productivity is relatively higher. Lastly, in estimating the supply-side impact of investment in a particular sector it is necessary to take into account factors like learning by doing, the potential for technological advances and spill-over effects. The last two considerations were extensively invoked to justify overwhelming emphasis on industrialization and the relative neglect of agriculture in the 1940s and 1950s. This development strategy, of course, cannot wholly be successful in all cases. Albert Hirschman in his important book: "*The Strategy of Economic Development*", has much to say in this respect.[22]

Some development economists attach under-importance to savings as a means of promoting economic growth. This has been criticized. The rational expectations school, as represented by Neil Wallace, Thomas Sargent, Robert Lucas and others, has made an interesting observation. These economists have questioned the ability of the government to raise aggregate savings when household can anticipate the impact of government. policies on future income streams and adjust there savings accordingly. Robert Baro[23], William Buiter and James Tobin[24] have also pointed out that household savings may not be a crucial factor in capital formation. Robert Solow wrote two important articles, one in 1956 and the other in 1957[25]. In the first article he showed that an increase in the savings ratio provides only a temporary rather than a permanent boost to the rate of economic growth. In the second article he showed that empirical studies of year-to-year changes in the domestic products suggest that only a small part of growth can be explained by capital accumulation or increases in employment. The larger unexplained part, known as Solow residual, is attributed to technological improvement and underlines the importance of factors other than savings in providing a lasting stimulant to economic growth. In trying to raise savings rate many developing countries have neglected the allocative efficiency, improvement in the quality of labour force and advancement of technological capacity-factor that came to be recognized by the mid-1970s as the most important determinant of economic growth.

Two economists who contributed substantially to development economics are Rosenstein-Rodan and Nicholas Kaldor. In college level text-books we can find some discussion about Rodan. But Nicholas Kaldor does not figure at all. Rodan advocated for the strategy of unbalanced growth. His 'Big-Push' theory is well-known. Rodan was a believer in investment planning, and he talked about what is technically known as its 'threshold effects'. In 1960 he wrote an important paper named '*Notes of the Theory of Big-Push*'.[26] Here he criticized the simple gradualist approach to development problem. In gradualist approach economic decision is taken and justified on the margin—a somewhat neo-classical way of thinking. This approach, according to Rodan, would not be successful in this context. Instead we should focus attention on the problem of complementarities in production as well as consumption planning. In consumption theory stress is laid on the role of hierarchical structure of wants. When formalized, this would generate a number of contemporary themes in the theory of choice and demand. Similarly the concept of 'basic needs' would come to the surface. This concept gained some significance in development literature during the mid-1970s. According to Rodan the existence of surplus labour in LDCs is helpful for development. But this would help only when surplus labour is galvanized by injecting fresh capital of sufficient magnitude, most probably imported from abroad. In this manner a process of productive transformation of backward countries like India and China could be initiated. This view he expressed in an important article entitled 'The International Development of Backward Areas.'[27]

Nicky Kaldor's primary object was to find out how far Keynesian economics could be applied to analyzing problems of long-run growth. His theory of economic development is a by-product of that endeavour. Kaldor argues that agricultural surplus plays a key role in the early phases of industrial development of low income countries. Such surplus creates employment opportunities in the non-agricultural sectors of the economy. Surplus agricultural produce provides for the growing real wage bill in the non-agricultural sectors. It also provides a growing market for industry. The growth of effective demand for industrial products due to increased volume of marketed surplus could turn into an upward cumulative process. The prevalence of increasing returns in industry helps in this process. The view that increasing returns playing a strategic role in the growth process is generally not acceptable to many economists. They are hesitant because the notion subsumed several disparate items, such as static and dynamic externalities as well as the influence of indivisibility on the choice of production process. It is well-known that significant increasing returns to scale often create intractable problems for applying conventional equilibrium theoretic reasoning. Kaldor had rather strong reservations about the relevance of equilibrium economics.[28]

Kaldor's theory of development runs like this: in the initial phases of developing economics the agricultural surplus acts as a triggering mechanism, whereas for advanced economics net exports to be the driving force. He believed that in most backward economics while agriculture is generally supply constrained, especially because land is often a limiting factor, industrial expansion is typically demand constrained. Prevalence of increasing returns in industry implies that the typical industry cost curve has a large flat segment. As a result industrial prices are usually cost-determined with mark-up varying according to the nature and extent of competition, which is necessarily imperfect.

Kaldor said that for a cumulative process to term into a structural transformation process, agriculture must be sufficiently responsive to outside forces, and the peasantry especially must be market-oriented in its behaviour. Land reform is an important factor in promoting agriculture since it encourages agricultural innovation, favourable export to the rest of the world could help, provided judicious support is advanced by the state in the form of suitable subsidies, or protective tariffs.

Many economists are quite skeptical about the quality and relevance of development economics, particularly of its theoretical constructs and its policy prescriptions. For instance, Jagadis Bhagwati argues that the so-called 'Marked-Failure' argument of development theory is limited and faulty because it puts undue emphasis on this as prime cause of economic stagnation. The elasticity pessimism feature of underdevelopment is also found to be an incorrect generalization from inter-war experiences. Nevertheless, Bhagwati takes a pragmatic stance and says there is still a role for development economics. The stark fact of poverty in LDCs is an eyesore. This has to be tackled by adopting correct economic policies, and here economists have a responsibility for formulating such policies. But this does not mean that market altogether has no part to play. Market, though imperfect, can play part, but only a limited part. And it is because of that the state needs to intervene in some cases. But this intervention must be selective in some targeted areas, and not wholesale nationalization of industries.

Albert Hirschman's position in regard to development economics is somewhat ambivalent. He wrote an illuminating essay aptly called *The Rise and Decline of Development Economics.*[29] Here he says "our sub-discipline had achieved its considerable luster and excitement through the implicit idea that could slay the dragon of backwardness virtually by itself or, at least that its contribution to this task was central. We now know that this is not so."[30] There is some plausibility in this diagnosis, but is it really true that development economics has no central role to play in the conquest of underdevelopment and economic backwardness? Can we say with any degree of certitude that the original themes with which development economics started are all untrue or useless? Amartya Sen does not think so. In his essay on "Development: which Way Now?"[31] he says that Hirschman's obituary lament for development economics is rather premature. The traditional development literature is indeed incomplete in coverage. But certainly it is not entirely pointless. The discipline of development economics does definitely have a central role to play in understanding the poverty of nations. Hirschman in his essay recognized the thematic similarities of the overwhelming majority of contributions in development economics. His own critique of the literature is highly scholarly and may be special subject for an independent essay. To economize time and space we do not enter into that domain. In criticism of Hirschman's position we just mention that there are some economists like Peter Bauer and Theodore Schultz—both conservative economists who stood outside of what is called standard development economics. Peter Bauer named his famous book: *Dissent on Development,*[32] just to indicate that he does not intend to jump on the bandwagon and join the obituary meeting of development economics.

Let us now take up Sen's own position. Though he admits that traditional development economics has much life left in the field of analysis of growth yet it has been much less successful in characterizing economic development. Growth and development, according to Sen, are not synonymous terms. He defines economic development as 'expansion of people's capabilities'. He then goes on to argue that if the development issues, in his sense, were to be usefully discussed, we would need to bring into focus what he calls the 'entitlement approach'. Sen's emphasis on the entitlement approach is well-known from his work on famines and poverty. As Sen's definition of entitlement is not tied exclusively to market type arrangements, he argues that we need to go beyond purely economic arguments.

Joan Robinson once said that in economics any new theory is a rediscovery. How true is this statement for a social science like economics. The distinction that Sen makes between growth and development has earlier been made by Schumpeter[33] and Lewis.[34] Schumpeter drew the distinction between the two in qualitative terms, or as some would like to say, in terms of a 'structural break'. He did not bring peoples capabilities into the analytical framework. But Lewis did. In the appendix to his book: *The Theory of Economic Growth*,[35] he said 'The case for economic growth is that it gives man greater control over his environment, and thereby increases his freedom.' Much later Sen wrote a book called *Development as Freedom*.[36] Isn't interesting? The Harvard philosopher John Rawls's book *Justice as Freedom*[37] might as well have its influence on Sen. Lewis's emphasis on freedom reveals that he was aware of the dimension raised by Sen. But his approach was production-centred and emphasized 'Man-nature' relationship while Sen's approach seems to turn around 'man-man' relationship. Lewis defined 'development economics' as the economics of countries with average per capita income below US $ 2,000 per annum. Some economists have ridiculed this definition. Lewis, however, made a distinction between the short-run/medium run problems of LDCs and their long-run problems. In the case of short-run problems, the differences are one of degree, rather than kind. These are well known cases of externalities, wage differentials, immobility of commodity markets etc. Lewis also provided a long list of new models invented by development economists. So far as long-run growth is concerned, Lewis said that there is not one growth theory but a set of complementary theories. He emphasized the need for careful research on government, class formation, class conflict and entrepreneurship.

We may now ask a few questions. Do Lewis's arguments constitute a reply to Hirchman's skepticism? Is Sen's analysis a useful approach to questions of poverty which, as Bhagwati avers, may not be fully taken into account by the market? Chakravarty raised these questions,[38] but he handled them from an ideological point of view, rather than purely economic.

Taking a pragmatic view, we find that our past experience of the last half century tells us that the 'market-failure paradigm' or simple Rostow type 'stages of growth argument' does not fully capture the causes of underdevelopment. For a better understanding of the problems we need to use a broader socio-anthropological framework. This, in other words, means that, apart from taking the scarcity view of economics, we have to consider the welfare aspect as well. Economics then becomes a subject which deals with 'social provisioning of goods and services'. To develop such a framework we have to take into account a few factors. The impact of economic organizations that generates creativity of the people, growth of the economy, and equity becomes important. Technological change, its proper use, and diffusion of its effects should form a part of the framework. In the context of development group interests are bound to arise. State action is needed here to lessen the tension. The world economic growth is uneven. In the context of internationalization of capital generates certain complications, different countries adopt different development strategies etc. All these dynamic factors must be incorporated in a generalized framework. To construct such a framework is not an easy job. Nevertheless, development economists must address themselves to this onerous task.

Up till now I have deliberately avoided an important aspect of development economics, viz. development strategies pursued by different countries. This aspect, of course, is important. Question like balance between (a) agriculture and industry, which is effectively the question of balance *versus* unbalanced growth strategy, (b) import-substituting industrialization under heavy industry strategy, (c) export-promotion strategy and so on are all discussed thoroughly in college-level text-books. Development strategies are born out of theoretical constructs. I have concentrated on some of the theories only.

The main points thrown up by development literature are, I think, as follows. In the first place we need to synthesize alternative paradigms so that we can understand the operation of the forces promoting or hindering economic development. Secondly, in order to effectuate this synthesis economist will have to judge the relevance of these paradigms against the historical experience of developing countries. Historical experiences of different countries are quite different. Lastly, economists should identify unresolved and newly emerging issues in development economics and chalk out lines of enquiry for their resolution. In recent years when the various LDCs have been adopting economic reforms of varying intensity and are feeling the impact of globalization new challenges are cropping up. They must be faced boldly and tackled efficiently. Some left-oriented critics tell us that the policy of so-called LPG, i.e. liberalization, privatization and globalization, is nothing but a disguised form of neo-imperialism inflicted by the developed West on Third World Countries. If there is even an iota of truth in this allegation, then this poses a serious threat. Environmental degradation and global warming, as a result of industrialization, also appear to be threatening. There is legitimate reason to apprehend whether mankind would ultimately survive in this sad, bad and mad world. Recently the Government of India has claimed that it is committed to pursuing a strategy that ensures growth process which is 'socially inclusive, regionally balanced and environmentally sustainable'. I am afraid; this may be a false claim. It is a semantic ploy, having no real substance. Our current history paints a dismal picture. I am sorry I have to end with this cynical note.

REFERENCES

1. M.G. Ranade: *Essays in Indian Economics*, (Madras, G.A. Watsan Co., 1906).
2. John H. Boeke: "Dualistic Economies", in W.E. Wertheim *et al.*, (ed.). *Indonesian Economics*, (The Hague, Von Hoeve, 1965).
3. Alfred Marshal, *Principles of Economics* (8th eds.), Landon: Macmillan, 1920.
4. Ragnor Nurkse, *Problems of Capital Formation in Underdeveloped Countries*, (Oxford: Basil Blackwell, 1953).
5. M. Kalecki, 'Review of M. Manoilesco', [*Economic Journal*, Vol. 48, No. 192, 1938, pp. 708-11].
6. Arthur Lewis, "*Economic Development with Unlimited Supplies of Labour*", [The Manchester School, Vol. 22, No. 2, 1954, pp. 131-91].
7. Arthur Lewis, "*Unlimited Labour: Further Notes*", [The Manchester School, Vol. No. 1, 1958, pp. 1-32].
8. Sukhomoy Chakravarty, "The State of Development Economics", a lecture delivered at the Manchester University, Department of Economics, on March 18, 1985. Reprinted in *Writings on Development*, (Oxford University Press, Calcutta, 1998).
9. J. Fei and G. Ranis, "Agriculture in the Open Economy", in E. Thorbecke (ed.) *The Role of Agriculture in Economic Development*, (Columbus University Press, 1969).
10. Avinas Dixit, "Growth Patterns in Dual Economy", *Oxford Economic Papers*, 1970.

11. Arthur. Pigou, *The Economics of Welfare*, (4th ed.) London, Macmillan, 1932.
12. P.N. Rosenstein-Rodan, "Problems of Industrialization in Eastern and South-Eastern Europe", *Economic Journal*, Vol. 53, no. 210, 1943, pp. 202-11.
13. Tibor Scitovsky, "Two Concepts of External Economics", *Journal of Political Economy*, Vol. 62, No. 1, 1954, pp. 143-51.
14. Sukhomoy Chakravarty, *ibid*, p. 180.
15. Raul Prebisch, "Five Stages in My Thinking on Development" in Gerald M. Meier and Dudley Seers (eds.), *Pioneers in Development*, 1984.
16. Jan Tinbergen, *The Design of Development*, Baltimore: The John Hopkins Press, 1969.
17. Prasanta Mahalanobis, (a) "Some Observations on the Process of Growth of National Incomes", *Sankhya*, Vol. 12, part 4, 1953, pp. 307-12. (b) "The Approach of Operational Research to Planning in India", *Sankhya*, Vol. 16, No. 2, pp. 30-62.
18. H.B. Chenery and M. Bouno, "Development Alternatives in an Open Economy: The Case of Israel", *Economic Journal*, Vol. 72, no. 285, 1962, pp. 70-103.
19. J.M. Keynes, "Economic Possibilities of Our Grand Children", in *Essays in Persuasion*, New York: W.W. Norton Co., 1963, pp. 358-373.
20. Roy Harrod: "An Essay in Dynamic Theory," *Economic Journal*, 49 (March 1939), 14-33.
21. D. Domar, "Capital Expansion, Rate of Growth, and Employment" *Econometrica*, Vol. 14, No. 2 (Apr., 1946), pp. 137-147.
22. Albert O. Hirschman, *The Strategy of Economic Development*. New Haven, Conn.: Yale University Press. 1958.
23. Robert Barrow: "Are Government Bonds Net Wealth?", *Journal of Political Economy*, 1974, 82 (6): 1095-1117.
24. Willem H. Buiter and James Tobin, 1978. "Fiscal and Monetary Policies, Capital Formation, and Economic Activity," in G.M. Von Furstenberg (ed.) *The Government and Capital Formation*, Ballinger, 1980.
25. (a) Robert M. Solow, "Contribution to the Theory of Economic Growth", *The Quarterly Journal of Economics*, Vol. 70, No. 1 (Feb., 1956), pp. 65-94 (b) "Technical Change and Aggregate Production Function", *The Review of Economics and Statistics*, Vol. 39, No. 3 (Aug., 1957), pp. 312-320 .
26. Paul Rosenstein-Rodan, "Problems of Industrialization of Eastern and South-Eastern Europe", *Economic Journal*, Vol. 53, No. 210/211, (1943), pp. 202-11.
27. ——"The International Development of Economically Backward Areas", *International Affairs*, V. 20 (1944) #2 (April), pp. 157-165.
28. *Nicholas Kaldor*, "The Irrelevance of Equilibrium Economics", 1972, *Economic Journal*.

29. Albert O. Hirschman: *Essays In Trespassing: Economics To Politics And Beyond*, Cambridge University Press, 1981.
30. Albert Hirschman, *ibid.* p. 23.
31. Amartya Sen, *Resources, Values and Development*, (Oxford University Press, Calcutta) (First Publishers in 1981 by Basil Blackwell Publishers Ltd., Oxford, England). Essay no. 19.
32. Peter Bauer, *Dissent on Development*, (London: Weidenfold and Nicolson, 1981).
33. Joseph Schumpeter, *The Theory of Economic Development*, (1912). The English edition, Somewhat revised, was published in 1934.
34. W. Arthur Lewis, *The Theory of Economic Growth*, (Richard D. Irwin, INC. Homewood, Illinois, 1955).
35. W. Arthur Lewis, *op. cit.*, p. 421.
36. Amartya Sen, *Development as Freedom*, (Oxford University Press, New Delhi, 2000).
37. John Rawls, *Justice as Freedom*, (Cambridge, Mass Harvard University Press).
38. S. Chakravarty, *op. cit.*, p. 194.

2

Disquieting Issues of Development in Developing Countries: An Analysis with Reference to India

Raj Kumar Sen

Introduction

Since the decolonization of the world after the Second World War, development has become the buzzword in the socio-economic discourses of the various independent countries in the context of their own socio-economic and geographical perspectives at a particular point of time. This was because the people in such countries aspired eagerly to achieve the standard of living enjoyed by their erstwhile rulers and they felt this will be achieved very soon after they became independent. Historically also there was an awareness that the colonies were very poor and this was made possible mainly due to exploitation and plunder by the imperialist countries as vividly noted in 'drain theory' by Dadabhai Naoroji and many others in pre-independent India. This was no exception for other similar countries also. The seminal writing by Colin Clark in 1940 about the sharp division in the level of GDP and per capita income between the imperialist countries and colonies put the problem of low income at the focal point of priorities fixed by the newly independent economies. In those days such economies were regarded as underdeveloped ones the features of which are well-known to everybody from many standard text books on development economies. Moreover the yardstick of development was primarily considered as the level of per capita income in comparable units and therefore, the governments tried to maximize their respective levels of per capita income as quickly as possible and also at the maximum possible rate. We find in the 1950s and 1960s that there was no difference between economic growth and economic development and unfortunately this concept is deeply rooted in the mindset of the policy-makers of developing countries even today including India. This becomes evident when we observe that Indian planners are engaged in fierce debate on the rate of economic growth will reach at the end of the year at 7.2 per cent or 7.5 per cent without taking care about the content or distribution of this growth symbolizing the dominance of the 'growth only' paradigm. At the core of this strategy lies the theory of trickle down of benefits from the earners in the highest income deciles to the lowest ones. This policy has already met its failure in four decades (1950-1990) of Indian planning but during the last two decades since the beginning of economic reforms based on the triple strategies of Liberalization, Privatization and Globalization (LPG) on the implicit plea that the trickle down of benefits did not work due to the slow rate of growth (often called sarcastically the 'Hindu rate') that India experienced in the pre-reform days but now it will be successful as we expect a rate of 8 per cent to 9 per cent on average.

Things started to change since the early 1970s and took a definite turn since 1990 with the publication of the first Human Development Report (HDR) by the UNDP. It was being gradually felt by many throughout the world that economic development and economic growth are different concepts and should never be considered as synonymous. Though economic development is considered in short to be something plus economic growth of income, yet it became extremely difficult to define economic development as it meant differently to different people of the world. For this reason all countries at low and medium income levels considered themselves to come under the ambit of developing countries. The high income industrialized countries of the world began to call themselves as developed though there was no specific definition of this concept in the strict sense.

Since the publication of the HDRs, the UNDP began to categorize different countries into high, middle and low development groups. Here they attempted to measure human development (not economic development) through HD Index based on measures of a decent standard of living, a healthy and long life expressed through life expectancy and achievement of knowledge through school enrolment and adult literacy. But even these could not give us an idea of human development in a complete form. Towards this end gradually emerged concepts like Human Poverty Index (HPI) for rich and other countries separately, Gender Development Index (GDI) and Gender Empowerment Measure (GEM) to supplement HDI. Some of the recognized factors affecting human development like ethnic harmony and people's freedom are yet to be incorporated within the group of measures included in the HDRs. It is significant to note that the World Development Report (WDR) published by the World Bank since late 1970s was engaged in arranging the countries in ascending order of per capita national income in constant US$ had to change this practice from 1995 to alphabetical order of the countries implicitly accepting the fact that world development cannot be properly captured if we restrict ourselves to the measure by per capita income only.

Fall-out of Economic Reforms

In India since independence, if we try to identify the different economic epochs following a similar approach made earlier by Amiaya Kumar Dasgupta for economic theory, then the ushering of economic reforms in 1991 must be regarded as one of them, the other two being the partition of India along with beginning of economic planning (1947-1950) and in 1969 the nationalization of commercial banks. We have now just completed two decades since the official initiation of economic reforms and within this short period the country has experienced a number of major quantitative and qualitative economic and social changes throughout the length and breadth of this vast country inhabited by more than one-sixth of the humanity. In this sense this may be definitely considered as the main issue of development in recent times for India which also happens to be one of the largest developing economies of the world. Consequently it is also high time to assess the impacts of economic reforms on India as the major development issues.

In order to understand these impacts more adequately, it should be remembered here that economic reforms imply simultaneous impacts of three economic strategies under it, popularly called together LPG, viz. liberalization, privatization and globalization and it would be confusing to consider the policy of economic reforms in isolation without analyzing the impacts of its constituent strategies. A number of different disquieting impacts cropped up in this process are: neglect of agriculture and problem of food insecurity, negative impacts on environment, jobless growth and corporate-led industrialization, inequalities in income and wealth, lack of good governance and plethora of scams, decline in values and criminalization of politics, commoditization of women and other negative impacts, etc. Some international events like global warming are also related to it with consequent effects of climate change mainly in the tropical countries in India. As all these issues are closely connected with neo-liberal policies currently followed either directly or indirectly, naturally the solutions to these problems will also depend on the successful adoption of alternative development paradigms based on sustainable options of non-exploitative nature. The recent global meltdown has already signalled the inner contradictions of the globalization process under the neo-liberal strategies and it is only a matter of time when the pendulum of economic development will swing back to the pro-people pro-environment alternative policies.

This article has made an attempt to highlight some of the negative impacts of economic reforms in India as mentioned above. It has deliberately avoided the real and so-called positive impacts of it since they are well-known through official propaganda and mainstream media publicity though in most cases the success stories are overblown. It is also a fact that not more than 20 per cent of the billion plus Indian population could gain during the last two decades while the material conditions of the remaining 80 per cent have either deteriorated or did not improve by a comparable amount experienced by the beneficiaries.

Neglect of Agriculture and Food Insecurity Problem

Though India is still now an agrarian economy as more than 60 per cent of its workforce is still dependent on agriculture for their livelihood, yet the share of agriculture to GDP has fallen sharply and now it is less than 20 per cent only. This shows the gradual decline in the standard of living of the people depending on the agricultural sector as they are compelled to consume from a continuously declining pie. One of the greatest mistakes of economic reforms in India is the neglect of the agriculture and overemphasis on the tertiary sector. Even the manufacturing sector which is considered to be the backbone of any industrialized economy did not receive adequate importance and degenerated into undesirable pattern (discussed in the next subsection). Unfortunately the agricultural sector did not grow at the stipulated rate of at least 4 per cent annually and it has declined to a critical level at present to -0.25 per cent only according to the Economic Survey 2009-10 published by Government of India. Even a couple of years ago Indian economy could boast of self-sufficiency in food- grains and the government faced the problem of overflowing food godowns. But now India is facing the problem of food insecurity with falling per capita food availability. However, the situation for grams and pulses which are considered to be poor men's protein, has already faced acute scarcity in increasing degree since the days of green revolution as it bypassed these crops and was concentrated mainly for wheat and paddy. The impact of green revolution to enhance agricultural productivity has gone down continuously with increasing costs of fertilizer, pesticide and irrigation and continuous changing pattern of cultivation from subsistence food economy sustained by small and marginal farmers to others due to increasing inequality among the land owners. The government is already seriously considering to start a second green revolution with the given name of 'evergreen revolution' on not only similar but also on more sophisticated lines. Naturally, it has been compelled to import food-grains from abroad on the one hand and to face the recent problem of rapidly rising food prices unprecedented in the history of the Indian economy causing acute hardship for the common people.

Another factor responsible for the emerging food crisis is the decline in its per capita supply due to gradually increasing substitution of agricultural land for the cultivation of non-food crops for the production of bio-fuels as scientists are warning about the rapid exhaustion of fossil fuels and their role in accentuating global warming. Besides under economic reforms for the sake of increasing exports, more and more food crops are being substituted by plantation leading to further decline in food output. Also the serious neglect by the government for extension of sustainable irrigation through small and medium surface irrigation projects has led to the pitiable fact that after sixty years of planning, more than 50 per cent of arable lands are still dependent on monsoon leading to mono-crop agriculture. The food output could be nearly doubled within a few years by extending irrigational facilities to all such areas. Besides the continuous efforts of the authorities to create more and SEZ areas are also considerably contributing to the gradual decline in food output.

Negative Impacts on Environment

While India was accustomed with dealing environment in a holistic sense since the ancient days, the current emphasis on environment is western in character and of an *ad hoc* nature not properly integrated with the society and the economy. This also started only since 1972 Stockholm International Conference emphasizing the need to protect environment. In conventional mainstream Western economics, environment was mostly regarded as a free good and at the best the degradation of environment was regarded as external diseconomies as discussed by Pigou. During 1972-1990, concern for environment received growing importance in India to the official level but it could not touch the lifestyle of the common masses. But since 1991, the importance of environment took a back seat in various forms and in different fronts in India along with other developing countries for the sake of accelerating the rate of economic growth as far as possible. This tendency was accelerated since 1995 when the WTO came into existence with India as one of the founder members. On the one hand we note that in the interest of industry and/or international trade, the existing environmental laws are either amended and/or repealed in many cases (e.g. import of hazardous wastes in coastal and other regions, opening of sanctuaries for mining and other industrial activities, allowing foreign tourists in areas so far prohibited for them in the name of ecotourism or otherwise which increased bio-piracy etc.) and on the other the authorities turned blind eyes to the violation of such laws in the name of protection of employment, industry or trade. The low awareness of the general public about environmental priorities in developing countries like India has also contributed to this negative impact. The recent changes suggested for project clearance norms will put almost 90 per cent of the industrial projects exempted from the legal requirements of Environmental Public Hearing (EPH). In India, degradation of environment means adverse effects mainly on the rural people as their poverty is basically an ecological poverty determining their living standards. Both short and long term steps are necessary to meet the challenge of economic reforms on environmental laws. These include continuous effort to increase public awareness about the urgency of protection of environment, short term targets of plugging the loopholes in the existing environmental laws and to implement them effectively with adequate punishment for their violations. This is feasible in democratic countries like India where the opposition can play a determining role in preventing the existing scenario from further decline.

Jobless Growth and Corporate-led Industrialization

Another disquieting feature of this reform period has been the occurrence of jobless growth and the undesirable degeneration of the industrialization from entrepreneurship motivated to a corporate-led one. Though the economic reforms targeted to put India on the trajectory of a higher growth rate, yet in the first ten years of its operation there was no appreciable increase in this front compared with the previous decade of 1980s. It accentuated only in the first decade of the present century and especially during 2002-2006 when the GDP growth rate averaged from 6 per cent to 8 per cent per year. This rate also has come down to some extent since 2007 as a consequence of the global meltdown. But the most unfortunate part of this reform period is the feature of jobless growth where high growth rate of GDP was accompanied with the falling growth rate of employment, especially of regular type. In fact, in the pre-reform days, the GDP grew at only 4 per cent annually on average and the employment rate growth was 2 per cent per year which was about the rate of population growth. In the post-reform days while the GDP growth rate doubled to nearly 8 per cent per annum on average, the rate of employment growth came down to half of its previous level, i.e. to 1 per cent only far less than the labour force increase. This was due to the failure to transfer surplus labour from stagnant agriculture to other growing sectors, increasingly capital-intensive growth process in manufacturing and tertiary sectors due to rapidly increasing sophisticated technology, disinvestment of the PSUs which were the main source of employment generation in pre-reform days, stagnancy or even decline of employment in the private sector, expansion of working hours with the existing labour force without increasing the level of employment, impact of world depression in a number of export-oriented industries like textiles, gems and jewelleries, tannery and many others leading to loss of jobs to the tune of more than one million, etc. No steps were taken by the authorities either to increase the level of employment (which was also not possible under economic reforms as the government was withdrawing itself from economic activities as far as possible) nor the government did anything to help the jobless workers in the depression stricken sectors although it bailed out crores of rupees to the corporate sector for their survival and retention of their profit as far as possible. The jobless growth has been a predominant feature of most of the economies adopting the policy of economic reforms as mentioned in the HDR 1995. This feature leads to both ruthless and voiceless growth which ultimately degenerates into futureless growth. The increase in casual and temporary jobs substituting regular and permanent ones is also leading to late marriages and hampering the family system in the society.

In India, however, this problem has been accentuated due to the rapidly changing character of industrialization. On the one hand the manufacturing sector did not receive in this period the attention it deserves, and on the other it shifted its emphasis to the tertiary sector and especially to the IT industries. Moreover the role of the entrepreneurs in initiating the industrialization process has been hijacked in the reform era by the corporate sector including large MNCs, most of which have their headquarters in USA and other high income countries. As a consequence of this the industrialization has gone to various non-conventional areas like mining, cultivation for bio-diesel production and contract farming, promotion of various activities in SEZs and so on. This has led to devastating consequences especially in tribal dominated areas mostly in the heartland of India. It has been estimated that the tribals had to bear a disproportionately high share in terms of eviction from their homelands, loss of occupation and forest rights among the people who have been adversely affected due to the so-called development activities. In fact a new paradoxical term, development oustees, has emerged in economic literature to describe the plight of such people. Without having proper rehabilitation either from the corporate sector or from the state, these otherwise peaceful and relatively isolated tribal people have now fallen in the grip of the terrorists which has become now one of the most serious problems of the Indian economy and eating up the growth process itself. In fact as many as seven states and more than one-third of the total districts of central India which are the main source of India's mineral wealth, have now practically gone out of the administrative control. All these are directly related to the plight of the poor and tribal people adversely affected by the reform process.

Inequalities in Income and Wealth

Historically the global inequality is on the rise and it is rising rapidly since the beginning of the neo-liberal regime. It is estimated that in 1750 the countries of the world were nearly at par in terms of their income which became 1:4 in 1930 and 1:7 in 1980 showing a rise in inequality among countries. By any measure this ratio has become further skew during the last 30 years though there are debates about the exact figures. India is a land marked by inequalities of income and wealth since ancient days. But this has become an undesirable development issue in recent times due to the fact that this feature has scaled a new height in reform period not only in India but also in the world as a whole nearly crossing the tolerable limit. This has become evident from the fact that now the deposits in the Swiss banks have not been topped by rich countries like USA or Japan, but by poor India! Among the Indian states also the Gini coefficient has gone up from 0.175 in 1991-92 to 0.233 in 1998-99. In 2005, the value for India was 0.32 approximately which is higher than many countries of the world. Some of the reasons for this high and increasing level of inequality in India have been analysed in the previous sections of this article. We may highlight two more points in this context. First, Indian growth process since independence has always been inequality promoting as there was no policy for redistribution of additional income generated from additional investments or for reducing the current inequality and the process of trickle down of benefits from the top to the bottom (a policy on which India relied since the planning era and again since the beginning of economic reforms with renewed vigour) itself is inequality promoting as it permits the income flow (if anything is left at all) in the downward direction only after completely fulfilling the desires of the top income classes. Second, one of the major reasons why inequality did shot up since 1991 in a significant manner is the application of a truncated globalization process favouring capital and finance and discriminating labour. The gap between the capitalists and workers and also the urban-rural gap could not increase in the present manner if the globalization would have been a true one favouring equally all factor owners. This has been accelerated being complimented with the privatization strategy where the state is receding from its role of promoting the welfare of the weaker sections of the people.

Lack of Good Governance and Plethora of Scams

Corruption at all levels of the society is a distinct symptom of the lack of good governance for any country. India may be a country of lofty ideals but in practice it has been infested by rampant corruption since the ancient period as evident from Kautilya's observations in *Arthasastra*. But what is significant in the post-reform era is the liberalization of a plethora of scams starting from Harshad Mehta case in the early 1990s to the recent Satyam episode showing a deep malady in the Indian economy assuming highly undesirable proportions in the last two decades. Again this may be considered as only the tip of the iceberg as most of such scams remain unexposed and only the most major ones see the light of the day. It was really shocking as revealed in the last case where there was more than 20000 fake employees in the pay roll and it went unnoticed year after year by an internationally reputed auditor firm. India's position in the ranking of corruption as per the estimates of Transparency International is also quite alarming. The scope of international money transfer has been greatly increased with the advent of modern technology supporting the globalization of finance. The allocation under several welfare schemes by the government still fail to reach the targeted people (reaching only 15 paise per rupee as per the comments of a former Prime Minister of India) and with the increase of funds in such schemes the non-poor is more benefited than the poor. The politicization of the village panchayats and the allocation of huge funds to them without adequate monitoring and control measures have led to the proliferation of the corruption virus even to the remotest hamlets implicitly giving a social sanction to corruption making the problem much more difficult to tackle as economic crimes are no longer socially considered as serious ones. Unfortunately all measures officially adopted so far have proved to be ineffective to control corruption in this country.

Decline in Values and Criminalization of Politics

Decline in values as such may not be a matter of economics proper, thanks to the dictum of Lionnel Robins that economics should be neutral between ends, but we may be concerned about it when it affects the various economic aspects of the country. It is usually admitted that Indian social and moral values started to erode rapidly since the Second World War when concern about money became supreme over other considerations. However, our economic theories about the consumer and producer behaviour are also value neutral. In fact they are value eroding in the sense that the consumer is trying to shift the budget line to maximize his utility and the producer is trying to maximize his profit and in this process both are free to adopt any means independent of any ethical considerations. In neo-classical economics we are following Marshallian analysis of rationality but are neglecting his concern for morality from it. The situation has become more critical since the reform days as growth of income and income only became the sole criterion of success in every field of life. It is said that under reforms, market is the temple and money is the deity in it. In earlier days display of conspicuous consumption was considered as undesirable but now such constraints exist no more. This is well connected with the use of money in the election process of our country leading to criminalization of politics in India in recent times making democracy a farce. This has become evident when we observe tainted politicians still hold power and the law of land fail to bring them into book.

Commoditization of Women and other Negative Impacts

It is really a paradox when on the one hand we speak about empowerment of women and on the other we promote use of women to earn money through commoditization of their physical features. The current visual media is taking a big role in this process. The state is putting a blind eye to all these by blaming the market demand for such undesirable events.

Global Warming

We may conclude the discussion on development issues by considering one international event and its impact in addition to the different fallouts of economic reforms. Of course, this also can be indirectly related to the excessive fossil fuel consumption and overexploitation of natural resources which increased in recent decades under economic reforms. Further this problem is of recent origin in the current century and it was never heard of in the pre-reform days. Though nothing is proved in a conclusive manner as the impacts of global warming as these are results of small surveys in high income countries only and the decisions arrived at by the IPCC IV are also disputed. As it is claimed that the global warming impacts will take place mostly in tropical countries, more extensive surveys under official agencies need to be conducted to arrive at meaningful and reliable results. It is also observed that the international emphasis so far had been on deforestation only as the cause of global warming and the issue of fossil fuel consumption is quietly sidelined. Moreover the policy of carbon trading is mostly emphasized to protect the current consumption level of fossil fuels by the rich countries forgetting the heterogeneous character of global environment. The recent near failure of the Copenhagen Summit may serve as an eye-opener.

Concluding Remarks

A one line conclusion may be made at this stage. Since all the recent negative issues of development are the fallouts of the policy of LPG strategies, these can be mitigated only through substitution of such policies by alternative development paradigm based on holistic, sustainable and pro-poor and people friendly strategies. Till this is not possible, the developing countries should try to join together to face the challenge as they have done in WTO negotiations, strengthen the role of the state to control the market as far as possible, try to look for indigenous policies to protect own biodiversity and similar other policies. India being the largest democracy in the world and being one of the 12 mega-biodiversity regions has a special responsibility in leading the developing world to fight against the negative repercussions discussed above. Only an enlightened and empowered people can show the way to make the nations free from all such perverse forms of economic growth.

REFERENCES

1. Dasgupta, A.K. (1985): *The Epochs of Economic Theory*. Oxford University Press, New Delhi.
2. Govt. of India (2010): *Economic Survey 2009-10*.
3. Sen, Raj Kumar (2009): 'Truncated Globalization and Inequality in India'. *Artha Beekshan*, Vol. 18, No. 2.
4. ——'Climate Change and Human Development: HDR 2007-08'. Keya Sengupta (ed.) *Human Development: Multi-Dimensional Approach to Human Well-Being*. Concept Publishing Co. Pvt. Ltd., New Delhi.
5. Sen, Raj Kumar and Somnath Hazra (2010): 'Globalization and

Environmental Governance with special reference to India'. *Rabindra Bharati Journal of Economics,* Vol. IV.

6. Sen, Raj Kumar (2010): 'From Green to Evergreen Revolution in India'. *Artha Beekshan,* Vol. 19, No. 2 *(forthcoming)*
7. UNDP (1995): *Human Development Report, 1995.*

3

Globalization and Poverty: Experience of the SAARC Countries

Jayanta Sen

Globalization started around 1980s and became widespread and more pronounced in the world economy in the 1990s. Several countries have removed restrictions on trade, movement of capital and transfer of technology in order to integrate the domestic economy with the global economy. The present paper deals with the issue of globalization and poverty in the context of SAARC countries. An attempt has been made in this paper to identify the impact of globalization on incidence of poverty in the SAARC countries. Nature and extent of globalization and its relationship with poverty is analytically discussed.

The new phase of globalization started around 1980s and became widespread and more pronounced in the world economy in the 1990s. Several countries have proceeded towards the integration of domestic economy with the global economy in order to bring economic efficiency. Countries have removed restrictions on trade, capital movement and transfer of technology. There has been a rapid transformation of the world economy from its traditional nature to free and market based economy.

Issues of globalization and deprivation have received a great deal of attention during the last few years. Several studies support the positive association between globalization and growth (Lundberg & Squire, 1999; Doller and Kraay, 2001; Goldberg, 2004). But growth does not always ensure higher welfare (Doller and Kraay, 2001).

Studies are also concentrated on impact of globalization towards enlarging inter, country differences. Some are, however, concerned with wage and income inequality in various countries (Scott, 1999; Robertson, 2000; Sen & Pal, 2006). But this paper aims at identifying the impact of globalization on incidence of poverty in the SAARC countries. The objective of this paper is to examine the nature and extent of globalization and to identify the impact of globalization on poverty incidence in the context of SAARC countries.

Globalization: Conceptual and Measurement Issues

Globalization in general aims at integration of the domestic economy with the global economy. It envisages removal of restrictions on trade, capital movement and transfer of technology. Globalization translates into greater mobility of factors of production and greater world integration through trade and investments.

Liberalized multilateral trade system is very much conducive to growth (Harission, 1999; Doller and Kraay, 2004; Goldberg, 2004). More openness leads to growth by increasing investment, more port of capital goods, more employment generating background and forward linkages. More globalized market induces competitive pressure that leads to technical upgradation and efficiency in production.

Association between openness and growth does not confirm the decline of deprivation. Studies showed that globalization leads to an increase in wage and income inequality. Some studies are concerned with the fact that there will be less unequal income distribution in the less developed countries due to high mobility of factors of production. Stiglitz (1998), Hurrol and Wood argued that globalization lead to increase in inequality as trade openness increases differentials in returns of education and skill.

More globalized economy induces agricultural productivity, increases efficiency in production of goods and services and also increases consumption level of people through inflow of financial resources. Studies also support that growth is good for the poor (Doller & Kraay, 2001). Thus one may hypothesize that the economy with more openness, less will be its poverty level. It is reasonably expected that multilateral trade system is likely be able to reduce deprivation in absolute sense.

The extent of globalization may be explained through a number of parameters and economic indicators—

Trade openness: Openness in trade promotes growth, allocative efficiency, technological advancement and socio-economic development. Trade openness is basically a function of volume of trade, i.e. imports and exports of an economy. Thus share of exports plus imports to Gross Domestic Product (GDP) is considered as measure of trade openness (O_T), i.e.

$$O_{Tj'} = \frac{X_j + M_j}{GDP_j} \quad \ldots (1)$$

X_j : Export of *j*th country

M_j : Import of the *j*th country

GDP_j : Gross Domestic Product of jth country

Openness in Foreign Direct Investment (FDI): Foreign Direct Investment (FDI) has now become an important variable in stimulating the process of globalization. Inflow of capital improves the long-term outlook of a country by improving knowledge and technology. Recently FDI is a composite of capital, knowledge and technology. It creates positive externalities by creating new inputs and technology. Thus inflow of FDI is an important indicator of the extent of globalization in an economy. Thus Openness in FDI is denoted as

$$O_{FDI\,j} = \frac{F_j}{GDP_j} \quad \ldots (2)$$

F_j: Foreign Direct Investment in the *j*th country

GDP_j : Gross Domestic Product of *j*th country.

Simple average of two openness indices (Trade and FDI) yield the Globalization Index (G_L) which captures the extent of globalization in an economy as

$$G_{L_j} = \frac{1}{2}\left(O_{T_j} + O_{FDI\,j}\right) \quad \ldots (3)$$

It is important to note that the index attaches the same weight to two openness indices. Several weighting schemes may be used to yield alternative weighted indices. To put equal emphasis and to make it simple we have used simple average in aggregation. More the value G_L, the economy will be more globalized. When the value is zero, the economy is perfectly closed economy. There is no international trade and foreign direct investment.

Poverty: Concept and Measurement Issues

A person is regarded as poor if his income falls short of the amount (called the poverty-line) which is required to maintain minimum levels of living. Thus poverty refers to inability of the people to attain certain predetermined minimum consumption needs. Standard of living of the people under poverty has quite different compared to the people above the poverty line (affluent group).

Measurement of income poverty requires the income distribution and the reference income called the poverty line income. In measuring poverty three questions crop up. (i) How many persons have income less than the poverty-income? (ii) How intensely are persons affected by poverty? (iii) Are poverty sufferings equally distributed? Question (i) refers to poverty incidence, question, (ii) to poverty intensity and question and (iii) to poverty distribution.

Consider an economy having N persons whose incomes are arranged in non-decreasing order as $y_1 \leq y_2 \leq \ldots \leq y_N$. Suppose, $y_i < y^*$, $i = 1, 2, \ldots, n$ where y^* is poverty income. Then incidence of poverty is

$$H_P = n/N \qquad \ldots (4)$$

$0 \leq H_p \leq 1$. It ignores the income gaps which captures the distance between income/consumption of individuals from the poverty line. Poverty intensity index (Ip) is another measure of poverty deals with average poverty gap, i.e.,

$$IP = \frac{1}{y^*} \sum_{i=1}^{n} gi/n ; g_i = y^* - y_i \qquad \ldots(5)$$

Where g_i the poverty gap of the i th poor.

Severity of poverty (S_p) which is sensitive to the poverty gap

(Sen, 1976) is measured in terms of H_p, I_p and Gini-coefficient (G_p) of the income of the poor as

$$S_p = H_p\left[I_p + \left(1 - I_p\right)G_p\right] \qquad \dots (6)$$

Foster, Greer and Thorbecke (1984) have used the coefficient of variation in their measure of inequality and defined the Severity Index:

$$FGT_p = H_p\left[I_p^{\,2} + \left(1 - I_p\right)^2 CV_p^{\,2}\right] \qquad \dots (7)$$

$CV_p^{\,2}$ is the squared coefficient of variation among the poor.

Absolute Deprivation and Globalization Indicators

From the above discussion it follows that absolute deprivation/poverty is a function of two important indicators—per capita income and inequality in income distribution, i.e.,

$$D_{jt} = f\left(\mu_{jt,} G_{jt}\right) \qquad \dots (8)$$

D_{jt} : Incidence of absolute deprivation/poverty in the country *j* at the *tth* period

$\mu_{jt,}$: Per capita income of country *j* at the *tth* period

G_{jt} : Gini coefficient of the country *j* at the *tth* period

Change in poverty becomes $\Delta D_{jt} = f\left(\Delta\mu_{jt}, \Delta G_{jt}\right) \dots (9)$

Globalization variables have some impact on growth and distribution as argued by so many economists, we have discussed earlier. Thus we can write

$\mu_{jt} = \theta\left(O_{T\,jt}, O_{FDI_{jt}}\right)$ and

$$G_{jt} = \theta\left(O_{T_{jt}}, O_{FDI_{jt}}\right) \qquad \dots (10)$$

It thus follows $D_{jt} = \phi\left(O_{T_{jt}}, O_{FDI_{jt}}\right)$ and

$$\Delta D_{jt} = \phi\left(\Delta O_{Tjt}, \Delta O_{FDI_{jt}}\right) \qquad \text{... (11)}$$

So as $G_{L_{jt}} = f\left(O_{T_{jt}}, O_{FDI_{jt}}\right)$, we can write

$D_{jt} = \Psi\left(G_{L_{jt}}\right)$ and

$$\Delta D_{jt} = f\left(\Delta G_{L_{jt}}\right) \qquad \text{...(12)}$$

Increased openness in trade and FDI as per several studies highly associated with growth and distributional inequality. Globalization variables are highly correlated with growth. But whether the globalization indicators tend to reduce poverty or not is the point of interest. For this purpose following cross section regressions are used to identify the impact of globalization on poverty incidence:

$$D_{jt} = \lambda_1 + \lambda_2\, GL\, jt + u_{jt} \qquad \text{...(13)}$$

$$D_{jt} = \eta_1 + \eta_2 O_T + u_{jt} \qquad \text{...(14)}$$

$$D_{jt} = \beta_1 + \beta_2 O_{FDI_{jt}} + u_{jt} \qquad \text{....(15)}$$

Empirical Results

The paper has attempted to identify the impact of globalization on deprivation in the context of SAARC countries. South Asia is as a region of poorest and overpopulated. More than one-sixth of the total labour force lives in South Asia. South Asian countries have low income, high density of population and poor health condition. In 1985, Bangladesh, Bhutan, India, Maldives, Pakistan, and Sri Lanka formed South Asian Association for Regional Cooperation (SAARC). The goal was to promote greater regional coordination on socio-economic issues. The countries also have gone through more economic integration in terms of free trade agreement. We have considered these countries to examine the extent of globalization and its impact on the poverty level.

Trade Openness in SAARC Countries

The degree of trade openness has varied widely across SAARC countries. Degree of openness in Maldives and Sri Lanka is higher compared to other countries. It is also fluctuating over different time periods. It has continuously increasing in case of India and Bangladesh. Sri Lanka and Maldives have performed better trade openness (Table 1).

Table 1: Trade Openness in SAARC Countries 1991-2004

Countries	*Trade Openness Index (O_t)*			
	1990-91	*1994-95*	*1999-2000*	*2003-04*
Bangladesh	0.1722	0.2398	0.2828	0.3148
Bhutan	0.5281	0.7604	0.6398	0.5792
India	0.1480	0.2132	0.2282	0.2580
Maldives	—	0.7962	0.7444	0.8450
Nepal	0.2354	0.3872	0.4322	0.3986
Pakistan	0.3374	0.2428	0.2782	0.3206
Sri Lanka	0.5730	0.7054	0.8658	0.7758

Source: Computed from World Development Reports and World Development Indicators.

In case of Nepal and Bhutan degree of trade openness has decreased. In case of India, Pakistan and Bangladesh the progress of openness is very slow. In case of India trade openness varies from 14 per cent in 1990-91 to 16 per cent in 2003-04. In case of Sri Lanka it is 57 per cent to 77 per cent. Maldives has the highest openness. Sri Lanka comes in the second position and India stands in the last position. Extent of globalization is increasing. Maldives records a declining trend. In case of Nepal and Sri Lanka it is fluctuating.

Openness in FDI in SAARC Countries

Openness in Foreign Direct Investment (OFDI) as measured by FDI-GDP Ratio has increased in all the countries except Nepal and Pakistan during 1991-2000 (Table 2). Bangladesh, India and Sri Lanka show higher achievement in terms of FDI openness. We find that Bangladesh has improved a lot in terms of foreign direct investment after the year 1991.

Extent of Globalization in SAARC Countries

Extent of globalization as measured by the average of trade openness and openness in FDI depicted in Table 3. From the table it is observed that the extent of globalization has increased in all the countries except Pakistan. Extent of globalization which is measured by openness in trade and FDI is highest in Sri Lanka and lowest in Nepal in 1999-2000.

Table 2: Openness in FDI in SAARC Countries 1991-2000

Countries	*FDI Openness Index (O_{FDI})*	
	1990-91	*1999-2000*
Bangladesh	0.0	0.6
India	0.1	0.6
Nepal	0.2	0.1
Pakistan	0.6	0.5
Sri Lanka	0.5	1.1

Source : Computed from Would Development Reports and World Development Indicators.

Table 3: Globalization Index in SAARC Countries 1991-2000

Countries	*Globalization Index (G_i)*	
	1990-91	*1999-2000*
Bangladesh	0.0861	0.4414
India	0.1240	0.4141
Nepal	0.2170	0.2661
Pakistan	0.4687	0.3891
Sri Lanka	0.5345	0.9829

In 1991, Sri Lanka has exhibited the highest degree of globalization followed by Pakistan and Nepal. Bangladesh has the lowest rank. In 1999-2000, Rank of Sri Lanka has remained the same whereas Bangladesh and India replaced Pakistan and Nepal. Increase in the degree of globalization is very much pronounced in Sri Lanka, Bangladesh and India to some extent. Sri Lanka, India and Bangladesh have shown an improvement in this regard.

Globalization and Poverty in SAARC Countries

Deprivation means shortfall. Shortfall may be judged in terms of income, assets, capabilities and the like. Any shortage of income from a stipulated level of income which is needed to maintain a minimum standard of living referred as absolute deprivation. Poverty is a global problem and UNDP put its major goal to eradicate poverty and hunger from the world. High percentage of people in the underdeveloped and developing countries is living below the poverty line.

Poverty is a major problem in some South Asian Countries. It is widely dispersed across regions, across rural-urban areas. Economists argue that more openness in trade and investment benefits each and every sector of the society which It brings about a strong linkage effect. It is quite expected that more globalized the economy less will be the poverty level. Poverty in SAARC countries is depicted in Table 4. Head-Count Ratio measures the incidence of poverty (D). Head-Count Ratios (on the basis of 1 $ a day norm) show the poverty differentials among the selected SAARC Countries.

Table 4: Poverty in SAARC Countries: 1998

Countries	*Head Count Ratio or HCR*
Bangladesh	0.291
India	0.442
Nepal	0.377
Pakistan	0.310
Sri Lanka	0.066

Source: World Development Reports and World Development Indicators.

The incidence of poverty is highest in India, followed by Nepal, Pakistan and Bangladesh. Poverty is more than 30 per cent in India, Nepal and Pakistan. It is more than 20 per cent in Bangladesh. Sri Lanka has the lowest poverty ratio.

To examine the impact of globalization on poverty in the context of SAARC countries, we have regressed globalization index on poverty index (Head count ratio). Regression yields:

$$D = 0.528 - 0.462\, G_L \qquad R^2 = 0.8210$$
$$(7.59) \qquad (-3.71)^* \qquad R^{-2} = 0.7610$$

* significant at 5 per cent level

Regression coefficient is negative and statistically significant. It implies more globalized the economy less will be the incidence of poverty. In the SAARC countries we find that openness in trade and investment have a positive impact towards the reduction of poverty. Correlation coefficient between G_L and D is very high (0.9).

Regressions [equations (14) and (15)] of components of globalization yields:

$$D = 0.496 - 0.462\, O_T \qquad R^2 = 0.7697$$
$$(6.88) \quad (-3.17)^* \qquad R^{-2} = 0.6930$$

$$D = 0.476 - 0.462\, O_{FDI} \qquad R^2 = 0.597$$
$$(4.91) \quad (-2.11)^* \qquad R^{-2} = 0.463$$

* significant at 5 per cent level

Both the coefficients are negative and significant. Volume of export and import as a percentage of GDP is negatively related to the incidence poverty. More trade openness implies more growth and low poverty level. Similarly high foreign direct investment leads to a reduction in poverty. Thus foreign direct investment and trade openness in SAARC countries have positive role towards reduction in absolute deprivation.

Concluding Remarks

Degree of trade openness in Maldives and Sri Lanka is relatively higher compared to other SAARC countries. Bangladesh, India and Sri Lanka show higher achievement in terms of FDI openness. An improvement in the extent of globalization is observed in Sri Lanka, India and Bangladesh after 1990s. It is observed that higher degree of globalization implies higher growth and lower level of poverty. In the SAARC countries we find the positive role of openness in trade and foreign direct investment towards the reduction in poverty incidence.

REFERENCES

1. Doller, D. and Kraay, A. (2001). "Growth is Good for the Poor", *World Bank Policy Research*, 2587, World Bank.

2. Goldberg, L. (2004). "Financial Sector FDI and Host Countries: New and Old Lessons, *NBPR*, 1044.
3. Lundberg and Squire (1999). Inequality and Growth: Lessons for Policy Makers, The World Bank.
4. Robertson, R. (2000). "Trade Liberalisation and Wage Inequality: Lessons from the Mexican Experience", *World Economy*, Vol. 23, N6.
5. Sen, J. and Pal, D.P. (2006). "Can Educational Expansion Reduce Income Inequality? An Analysis of the Rural Economy of Southern India in the Capability-Accessibility Framework" presented in the *Annual Conference of Indian Economic Association held at Kuruksetra University*, Haryana during Dec. 27-29, 2006.
6. Stiglitz, E. Joesph (2002). *Globalization and Its Discontents*, Penguin Books, India.
7. Wood, A. (1995). "How Trade Hurt Unskilled Workers", *Journal of Economic Perspectives*, Vol. 9, No. 3.

4

Liberalization and Child Labour: Study of Welfare in Small Open Economy

Anindita Basu (Chowdhury)

Introduction

In recent years, particularly after globalization, the issue of child labour and its eradication and prevention has been considered as one of the most important issues facing the policy-makers of developing countries. In 1999 and 2000, UNICEF interviewed children across 30 developing countries. UNICEF discovered that a few number of children are engaged in the factory work. Unpaid domestic work is more common than work for pay. However, most working children are employed in their own household. ILO estimates that in 2000 about 211 million children aged 5-14 years old were engaged in some form of economic activity globally. Of these only 25 million were acceptable by the standard set by various ILO conventions and recommendations (mainly light work by children aged 12-14 years old). It is beyond any doubt that the main cause of this incidence of child labour is abject poverty, which compels people to have large families and children to go out in the job market and earn their own means of livelihood. Authors who have addressed this issue include Grootaert (1998) and most recently, Basu and Van (1998). They have emphasized on the link between households' struggle to survive and the incidence of child labour. Basu and Van (1998) have shown that if child labour and adult labour are substitutes[1] and if child labour is a luxury commodity[2] to the poor households, unfavourable adult markets are responsible for low adult wage rate and this is the main cause behind the incidence of child labour.

To eradicate the incidence of child labour, World Development Report 1995 called for a multifaceted approach with programmes that increase income securities, reduce education cost and improve the quality of schooling. However, due to various bottlenecks it is very difficult to implement these properly in a developing country. However, a total ban of child labour would be counter-productive in the sense that it may adversely affect the welfare of poor household and force the children to take more hazardous and illegal activities. Social labelling is not only difficult to operate but also it may have disastrous consequences on the developing economies as the recent Bangladeshi experience[3] has shown. Eswaran (1996) has suggested that improvement in healthcare services and legislation of compulsory education in the developing economies can reduce the level of child labour in these economies. On the basis of study of a city in western India, Swaminathan (1998) has concluded that liberalized trade policies and free education policy cannot successfully eradicate the problem of incidence of child labour. Dessy (2000) has argued that the promotion of human capital, which is the main constraint of poor countries, is an important measure for reducing incidence of child labour. Chaudhuri (2000) has also examined the implications of an education subsidy and removal of tariff restrictions on child labour. There is a theoretical literature including Ranjan (2001), Baland and Robinson (2000) and Jafaray and Lahiri (2002), which emphasizes the importance of capital market imperfection as a contributing factor to inefficient child labour.

Analyzing the cross country data Cigno, Rosati and Guarcello (2002) have found that globalization can contribute to reduce child labour by increasing the returns to education. Dwibedi and Chaudhuri (2003) have found that a reduction in import tariff and/or an increase in the price of the export commodity put downward pressures on the child labour incidence while an inflow of foreign capital may accentuate the problem. Chaudhuri and Gupta (2004) have shown that the effect of trade liberalization on the incidence of child labour depends crucially on the relative factor intensities of the two sectors and the values of parameters of the system. Considering a three-sector general equilibrium framework with two informal sectors and a non-traded final commodity Chaudhuri and Dwibedi (2006) have found that a policy on education subsidy is more effective in comparison with the policy of economic growth with foreign capital inflow to eradicate the problem of the incidence of child labour.

The main motivation behind this study generates from the fact that in spite of few empirical works only a few theoretical works have been made to examine the impact of foreign capital inflow on the incidence of child labour. Unfortunately, the existing theoretical literature have not analyzed the impact of foreign capital inflow on the incidence of child labour in the presence of agricultural dualism, which is a common feature of a developing economy. The distinction between advanced and backward agriculture can be made on the basis of inputs used, economies of scale, efficiency and elasticity of substitution. Although Green Revolution has brought some revolutionary changes with respect to production technologies and modern inputs use and the increase in factor productivity but it has been limited only to a few parts of a developing economy like India and only rich farmers have been benefited from this modern technology. Many of the small and marginal farmers in the agricultural sector of a developing economy like India are compelled to use old and unscientific methods of cultivation. Most of the existing literature have considered child labour as an input of formal agriculture and non-traded intermediate goods sector. But from empirical point of view it has been found that a large proportion of child labour have been engaged in this backward agricultural sector. In the present paper we have tried to capture this point. Apart from this in the present paper, unlike most of the works in the literature, we have considered domestic capital and foreign capital as imperfect substitutes and they are treated as separate inputs.

The present paper attempts to examine the effects of foreign capital inflow on the incidence of child labour and on the level of welfare in a developing economy in the Harris-Todaro (1970) framework in the presence of agricultural dualism. In this paper urban unemployment and migration of labour from rural (agricultural) sector to urban (manufacturing) sector on the basis of Harris-Todaro (1970) migration mechanism has been considered. Child labour has been assumed to be used in the agricultural sectors, which are divided into two parts, namely advanced agricultural sector and backward agricultural sector. In other words, child labour is perfectly mobile between the advanced agricultural sector and backward agricultural goods producing sector. The labourers working in the urban sectors (manufacturing sector and foreign enclave) earn wage income greater than the competitive equilibrium level and therefore they do not send their children to the job market. On the other hand labourers working in the other two sectors send their children to the job market in order to supplement their low income. Here we explore the possibility of reduction in the incidence of child labour and welfare improvement due to inflow of foreign capital, with full repatriation of its earning. Additionally we also explore the possibility of tradeoff between increase in welfare and increase in urban unemployment as a result of foreign capital inflow.

The plan of the paper is as follows: Section 2 specifies and explains the working of the model. The comparative static analysis regarding the effects of increase in foreign capital inflow of the above model is considered in the Section 3, Finally the concluding remarks are made in Section 4.

The Basic Model

We consider a small open less developed economy consisting of four sectors in a Harris-Todaro (1970) framework. There are two types of labour available in the economy: adult labour (L) and child labour (C). All these four sectors use adult labour which is perfectly mobile among these four sectors. Chlid labour (C) has been considered as mobile only between two domestic agricultural sectors, namely advanced agricultural sector, sector-A and comparatively backward agricultural sector, sector-B. Domestic capital (K_D) has been considered as mobile between domestic manufacturing sector, M, and the advanced agricultural sector, A. Foreign capital (K_F) on the other hand has been considered as specific to the foreign enclave. Here the advanced agricultural sector, A, produces its commodity (X_A) with the help of adult labour, child labour and domestic capital. The manufacturing sector, M produces its commodity (X_M) with the help of adult labour and domestic capital. The backward agricultural sector, B, produces its commodity (X_B) with the help of both types of labour only[4]. Here comparatively backward agricultural sector is assumed to be more child labour intensive compared to the advanced agricultural sector. The foreign enclave produces its commodity (X_F) with the help of adult labour and foreign capital. Here we assume that both the manufacturing sectors (domestic and foreign) are treated in the urban area and both the agricultural sectors are treated in the rural area. In the manufacturing sector and foreign enclave we find that due to the existence of unionized labour force the wage rate is fixed on the contractual basis at the level $\overline{w}$. Wages in the other two sectors are flexible and they are identical to the competitive wage rate w. Here contractual wage rate is assumed to be higher compared to competitive wage rate. In the model the existence of urban unemployment and migration from (rural) agricultural sector with lower wage to (urban) manufacturing sectors with relatively higher wage in a Harris-Todaro (1970) framework has been considered. Workers from the rural area (consisting of backward and advanced agricultural sectors) migrate to the urban area as long as the expected urban wage rate is higher than the rural wage rate. Migration stops when the two are equal. Owing to our small open economy assumption, we consider prices of all goods to be given internationally. The agricultural product is considered as numeraire and its price is set equal to unity. We assume that the manufacturing sector is the import competing sector and the agricultural sectors is the sector that produces exportable commodity. Production functions exhibit constant returns to scale with diminishing marginal productivity to each factor. The entire foreign capital income is assumed to be fully repatriated.

For specifying our model on the basis of the above assumption we use the following notations:

X_i = Product produced by the ith sector, $i = A, B, M, F$
P_i = World price of the ith commodity, $I = A, B, M$ and F
L = Fixed endowment of adult labour
C = Fixed endowment of child labour
K_D = Fixed endowment of domestic capital
K_F = Fixed amount of foreign capital
a_{ji} = Quantity of jth factor for producing one unit of output in the ith sector. $j =$ L, C, K_D, K_F, and $i = A, B, M, F$

w = Common adult wage rate of labour in all sectors
$\overline{w}$ = Contractual wage rate of the manufacturing sector and foreign enclave
w_c = Common wage rate of the child labour
r = Rate of return on domestic capital
r_F = Rate of return on foreign capital[5]
λ_{ji} = Proportion of jth factor used in the production of the ith sector
$\wedge$ = Proportional change
θ_{ij} = Distributive share of the jth input in the ith industry
Ω = A measure of welfare

The competitive equilibrium condition in the product market for the four sectors implies the following equations:

$$wa_{LA} + wca_{CA} + ra_{KA} = 1 \quad \dots (1)$$

$$wa_{LB} + wca_{CB} = P_B \quad \dots (2)$$

$$\overline{w}\, a_{LM} + ra_{KM} = P_M \quad \dots (3)$$

$$\overline{w}\, a_{LF} + rFa_{KF} = P_F \quad \dots (4)$$

Mobility of domestic capital can be expressed as

$$a_{KA}X_A + a_{KM}X_M = K_D \quad \dots (5)$$

The sector specificity of foreign capital is given by the following equation

$$a_{KF}X_F = K_F \quad \dots (6)$$

In this model the level of urban unemployment is denoted by U and urban unemployment rate is given by $\mu = U/(a_{LM}X_M + a_{LF}X_F)$

The migration equilibrium condition is stated as $\overline{w} = (1 + \mu)\, w$

Labour market equilibrium condition implies the following equation

$$(1 + \mu)(a_{LM}X_M + a_{LF}X_F) + a_{LA}X_A + a_{LB}X_B = L \quad \dots (7)$$

In this model each worker in the manufacturing sector and foreign enclave earns a contractual wage income $\overline{w}$ which is sufficiently greater than that critical level under which adult labourers are compelled to send their children out to work to supplement their low-income levels. So the labourers belonging to this group do not send their children to work and labourers of other two sectors, i.e. sectors A and B, send their children out to work to supplement their low-income levels. It has been assumed that each family has exactly one adult worker and certain number of children. Thus larger the number of adult labour in these two sectors, the larger would be the potential supply of child labour. Again supply of child labour is also a function of the child wage rate and also adult wage rate. Thus total supply of child labour is dependent on the adult wage rate of the two agricultural sectors, child labour wage rate and the number of representative families who send their children to the job market to supplement their low-income[6].

Total supply of child labour is given by

$$C = f(w, w_c, L_e) \qquad \ldots(8)$$

where $L_e = (L - a_{LM}X_M - a_{LF}X_F)$. Here $f_1 = (\partial f/\partial w)<0, f_2 = (\partial f/\partial w_c)>0$ and $f_3 = (\partial f/\partial L_e)>0$

Demand supply equilibrium in the child labour market is given by

$$a_{CA}X_A + a_{CB}X_B = C$$

$$\therefore \quad a_{CA}X_A + a_{CB}X_B = f(w, w_c, L_e) \qquad \ldots(9)$$

Where $L_e = (L - a_{LM}X_M - a_{LF}X_F)$

There are 10 endogenous variables in the system $w, w_c, r, r_F, \mu, X_A, X_B, X_M, X_F, C$. Here we have 9 independent equations (from equations 1 to 9) and migration equilibrium condition to solve for 10 unknowns. Given P_M and $\overline{w}$ we can find out the value of r from equation (3) and the value of r_F from equation (4). It is to be noted that once r is known then w and w_c can be obtained easily from equations (1) and (2). Once w is known we can easily determine the unemployment rate μ from migration equilibrium condition. Here the factor prices and the rate of unemployment can be determined independently of factor endowments. Thus the decomposability property is valid in our model. Hence we can solve the equilibrium values of the input-output coefficients. Once as a_{ij} are known and as K_F, K_D, and L are given, from equation (6) one can easily determine X_F as K_F is given. Again putting the value of X_F from equations (5),

(7), (8) and (9) we can solve the equilibrium values of X_A, X_B, X_M, C.

The Comparative Static Effects

In this section we want to examine the impact of foreign capital inflow on the level of child labour as well as national welfare of a developing economy. To do these at first we have to find out the effect of foreign capital inflow on the level of output of different sectors.

Differentiating equation (6) we can get $\hat{X}_F = \hat{K}_F$ ...(10)

Using the above result and differentiating equations (5), (7) and (9) we can get [see appendix for details]

$$\lambda_{KA}\hat{X}_A + \lambda_{KM}\hat{X}_M = 0 \quad \text{... (11)}$$

$$\lambda_{LA}\hat{X}_A + \lambda_{LB}\hat{X}_B + (1+\mu)\lambda_{LM}\hat{X}_M = -(1+\mu)\lambda_{LF}\hat{K}_F \quad \text{...(12)}$$

$$\lambda_{CA}\hat{X}_A + \lambda_{CB}\hat{X}_B + f_3\lambda_{LM}\hat{X}_M = -f_3\lambda_{LF}\hat{K}_F \quad \text{... (13)}$$

As w and w_c are independent of change in K_F due to the decomposability property the value of f_1 and f_2 are zero.

$$\therefore \hat{X}_A/\hat{K}_F = [\lambda_{KM}\{-(1+\mu)\lambda_{CB}\lambda_{LF} + f_3\lambda_{LF}\lambda_{LB}\}/|\lambda| \quad \text{... (14)}$$

$$\hat{X}_M/\hat{K}_F = [\lambda_{KA}\{-f_3\lambda_{LB}\lambda_{LF} + (1+\mu)\lambda_{LF}\lambda_{CB})/|\lambda| \quad \text{... (15)}$$

$$\hat{X}_B/\hat{K}_F = [\lambda_{KA}\{\lambda_{CA}\lambda_{LF} - (1+\mu)f_3\lambda_{LF}\lambda_{LA}\}/|\lambda| \quad \text{... (16)}$$

where $|\lambda| = [\lambda_{KA}(f_3\lambda_{LB}\lambda_{LM} - (1+\mu)\lambda_{LM}\lambda_{CB})] + [\lambda_{KM}(\lambda_{LA}\lambda_{CB} - \lambda_{CA}\lambda_{LB})]$

According to the assumption that B sector is more child labour intensive compared to the A sector, $(\lambda_{LA}\lambda_{CB} - \lambda_{CA}\lambda_{LB})$ is positive. Now $|\lambda|$ is positive under the sufficient condition $f_3 > (1 + \mu)\lambda_{CB}/\lambda_{LB}$.

It is to be noted that f_3 is the change in the supply of child labour as a result of a change in the number of families supplying child labour which is usually very high in developing economies. This is because of the tendency of the poor households to have more children. This ratio is not only more than one but also very high. Again $\lambda_{CB}/\lambda_{LB}$ is the proportion of child labour used in the production of the one unit of output of the B-sector compared to proportion of adult labour used in the production of one unit of same product. Though this ratio is more than one but its value is not so high. Again the value of $(1 + \mu)$ is nothing but the ratio of fixed manufacturing (urban) wage with respect to competitive equilibrium (rural) wage of adult labour which is also not so high. Thus the assumption that the change in the supply of child labour as a result of a change in the number of families supplying child labour deflated by the proportion of child labour used in the production of the one unit of output of the B-sector compared to proportion of adult labour used in the production of one unit of same product is greater than the wage ratio, i.e. $f_3 / (\lambda_{CB}/\lambda_{LB}) > (\overline{w}/w)$ appears reasonable.

Given the assumption $\lambda_{CB}/\lambda_{LB} > \lambda_{CA}/\lambda_{LA}$, i.e. sector-B is more child labour intensive (with respect to adult labour) compared to the sector-A, from equations (14), (15) and (16) we can say $\hat{X}_A / \hat{K}_F > 0$, $\hat{X}_B / \hat{K}_F < 0$ and $\hat{X}_M / \hat{K}_F < 0$ under the same sufficient condi-tion that $f_3 > (1 + \mu)\lambda_{CB}/\lambda_{LB}$.

Differentiating equation (8) we can get [see appendix for details]

$$\hat{C} / \hat{K}_F = \{f_3 (L/C) (\lambda_{LF}\lambda_{KM})(\lambda_{CA}\lambda_{LB} - \lambda_{LA}\lambda_{CB})\} / |\lambda| \quad \ldots (17)$$

Assuming $\lambda_{CB}/\lambda_{LB} > \lambda_{CA}/\lambda_{LA}$, i.e. sector-B is more child labour intensive (with respect to adult labour) compared to the sector-A, from equation (17) we can say that $(\hat{C} / \hat{K}_F)$ is negative under same sufficient condition $f_3 > (1 + \mu)(\lambda_{CB} / \lambda_{LB})$ which is quite a reasonable condition from the point of view of a developing economy.

An increase in foreign capital inflow, K_F, increases the output of foreign enclave, X_F. It causes a reduction in the supply of child labour. Again, an increase in K_F reduces the output of the manufacturing sector, X_M, under the sufficient condition $f_3 > (1 + \mu)\lambda_{CB}/\lambda_{LB}$ or $f_3 / (\lambda_{CB}/\lambda_{LB}) > (\overline{w}/w)$[7]. It causes an increase in the supply of child labour due to an increase in K_F. Finally, it can be shown from equation (17) that under the sufficient condition $f_3 > (1 +$

$\mu) \lambda_{CB}/\lambda_{LB} > \lambda_{CA}/\lambda_{LA}$, an increase in inflow of foreign capital reduces supply of child labour.

We next consider the impact of foreign capital inflow on the national welfare. Now we consider quasi-concave social utility function, denoted by U that depends on consumption demand for four final goods denoted by D_A, D_B, D_M and D_F and the number of child labour C, used in the two agricultural sectors. Thus it is shown as

$$U = U(D_A, D_B, D_M, D_F, C) \qquad \dots (18)$$

Taking total differential of equation (18) and the using the fact $(U_B/U_A) = P_B$, $(U_M/U_A) = P_M$ and $(U_F/U_A) = P_F$ (where $U_A = \partial U/\partial D_A$, $U_B = \partial U/\partial D_B$ and $U_M = \partial U/\partial D_M$ and $U_F = \partial U/\partial D_F$, $U_C = \partial U/\partial C < 0$) and $(U_C/U_A) = -\rho$ (where $U_C = \partial U/\partial C$) it is possible to write

$$d\Omega = dD_A + P_B dD_B + P_M dD_M + P_F dD_F - \rho dC \qquad \dots (18.1)$$

Here ρ measures the real social cost of child labour and $d\Omega = dU/U_A$.

Following Caves, Frankel and Jones (1996) we find that $d\Omega$ implies a measure of change in welfare measured in units of the product of sector- A. Here in the absence of tariff world price is equal to domestic price.

The trade balance equation requires that

$$D_A + P_B D_B + P_M D_M + P_F D_F = X_A + P_B X_B + P_M X_M + P_F X_F - r_F K_F \qquad \dots (19)$$

We know that $X_A + P_B X_B + P_M X_M + P_F X_F$ is the value of output measured at domestic price which is nothing but the value of $wa_{LA}X_A + wa_{LB}X_B + w(1+\mu)(a_{LM}X_M + a_{LF}X_F) + w_c C + r.K_D + r_F K_F$

$$X_A + P_B X_B + P_M X_M + P_F X_F = w.L + (\overline{w} - w).(a_{LM}.X_M + a_{LF}.X_F) + w_c C + r.K_D + r_F K_F \quad \dots (19.1)$$

Taking total differential of equation (19) we can get

$$dD_A + P_B dD_B + P_M dD_M + P_F dD_F = dX_A + P_B dX_B + P_M dX_M + P_F dX_F - r_F dK_F - K_F dr_F$$

Using equation (18.1) and also using equation (19.1) we get

$$d\Omega + \rho dC = wdL + Ldw + (\overline{w} - w).(a_{LM}.\, dX_M + a_{LF}.\, dX_F)$$

$$+(\overline{w} - w).(X_M da_{LM.} + X_F da_{LF}) +$$

$$(a_{LM.}X_M + a_{LF}X_F)(-dw) + w_c dC$$

$$+ Cdw_c + r.dK_D + K_{D.} dr$$

By decomposability property, when $dK_F>0$ we find that the factor prices remain unchanged so that $dw = dw_c = dr = dr_F = 0$. Again when $dK_F>0$, $dL = dK_D = 0$.

Thus $d\Omega + \rho dC = (\overline{w} - w).(a_{LM.} dX_M + a_{LF.} dX_F) + w_c dC$

$$\therefore \Omega(\hat{\Omega}/\hat{K}_F) = (\overline{w} - w).L.\ \{\lambda_{LM}(\hat{X}_M/\hat{K}_F) + \lambda_{LF}$$

$$(\hat{X}_F/\hat{K}_F)\} + C(\hat{C}/\hat{K}_F)(w_c - \rho)$$

As a result of foreign capital inflow we find that output of foreign enclave increases and the output of manufacturing sector and the supply of child labour decreases under the sufficient condition that $f_3 > (1 + \mu)(\lambda_{CB}/\lambda_{LB}) > (\lambda_{CA}/\lambda_{LA})$. A reduction in supply of child labour produces two opposite impact on welfare. On one side it produces a negative impact on welfare by reducing the total wage income of child labour which is represented by the term $w_c C(\hat{C}/\hat{K}_F)$, on the other side it produces a positive impact by reducing real social cost of child labour which is represented by the term $\{-C.\rho(\hat{C}/\hat{K}_F)\}$. Total expansion of formal manufacturing sectors has an impact on employment of adult labour of these two sectors. The workers of the two formal manufacturing sectors enjoy a wage rate $\overline{w}$, which is higher than the wage rate, w, in rest of the economy. The increase in employment in these two sectors is at the cost of reduction in employment in the rest of the economy. This is known as the labour reallocation effect due to a change in output (and hence change in employment) measured in terms of wage differential ($\overline{w}$-w). It is given by $(\overline{w} - w).\ \{a_{LM.}(dX_M/dK_F) + a_{LF.}(dX_F/dK_F)\}$. In other words, $(\overline{w} - w).\ L\{\lambda_{LM}(\hat{X}_M/\hat{K}_F)+\lambda_{LF}(\hat{X}_F/\hat{K}_F)\}$ measures the labour reallocation effect of foreign capital inflow on welfare. Under the sufficient condition $f_3 > (1 + \mu)(\lambda_{CB}/\lambda_{LB}) > (\lambda_{CA}/\lambda_{LA})$, $\{\lambda_{LM}(\hat{X}_M/\hat{K}_F)+\lambda_{LF}(\hat{X}_F/\hat{K}_F)\}$ is positive and so that this labour reallocation effect is also positive. Now the total welfare effect is dependent on the relative strength of these three effects. We thus find $(\hat{\Omega}/\hat{K}_F)$ is positive if the real social cost of child labour is greater than the wage rate of child labour i.e. $\rho > w_c$. Thus we have shown that in the Harris-Todaro (1970) framework where urban adult unemployment and migration of adult labour, from rural sectors to urban sectors has been considered, foreign capital inflow may produce a favourable impact on the incidence of child labour and national welfare.

Now we want to find out the impact of foreign capital inflow on the level of urban unemployment.

Total unemployment in the urban sector is

$$U = \mu\,(a_{LM}X_M + a_{LF}X_F) \quad \ldots (20)$$

Taking total differential of equation (20) we can get

$$dU = \mu(a_{LM}dX_M + a_{LF}dX_F)$$

$$\hat{U}\,U = L\mu(\lambda_{LM}\hat{X}_M + \lambda_{LF}\hat{X}_F)$$

$$\hat{U}/\hat{K}_F = \{\mu(L/U)(\lambda_{LF}\lambda_{KM})(\lambda_{LA}\lambda_{CB} - \lambda_{CA}\lambda_{LB})\}/|\lambda| \quad \ldots (21)$$

In order to find out the impact of foreign capital on the urban unemployment at first we need to find out the impact of such an inflow on the output levels of two urban sectors. From equation (21) we can say that an increase in foreign capital leads to an increase in the output of foreign enclave. Now from equation (21) we can say that foreign capital inflow produces a contractionary impact on the output of domestic manufacturing sector under the sufficient condition $f_3 / (\lambda_{CB}/\lambda_{LB}) > (\overline{w}/w)$. The two opposite effects on the output levels imply that the ultimate impact of foreign capital on urban unemployment is indeterminate. However given the assumption $\lambda_{CB}/\lambda_{LB} > \lambda_{CA}/\lambda_{LA}$ and same sufficient condition mentioned above we find that the level of urban unemployment increases. Thus we can summarize our results in the form of the following proposition.

Proposition: *In the presence of Harris-Todaro (1970) type urban unemployment and migration from rural to urban area, an increase in inflow of foreign capital with full repatriation of its earnings, reduces the incidence of child labour under the sufficient condition $f_3 / (\lambda_{CB}/\lambda_{LB}) > (\overline{w}/w)$. It also leads to an improvement in* *welfare if $\rho > wc$. Here we have also shown that the inflow of foreign capital increases the level of urban unemployment.*

Concluding Remarks

The impact of foreign capital inflow on the incidence of child labour and welfare of a small open economy is considered as one of the most important issues in the context of the developmental problems of a developing economy. The present paper shows that in the Harris-Todaro (1970) framework, in the presence of urban unemployment and migration of adult labour from rural area to urban area, foreign capital inflow may produce a favourable impact on the incidence of child labour and national welfare. Here we have shown that the level of urban unemployment increases due to foreign capital inflow.

Our result may encourage the policy-makers who are in favour of foreign capital inflow on the one hand and reduction of child labour on the other hand in developing countries. Our analysis, however, creates a trade off in front of the policy-makers of developing countries. On the one side an inflow of foreign capital increases national welfare (along with reduction of child labour), on the other side it increases the problem of urban unemployment of adult labour. This interesting issue can be resolved once we consider the empirical aspects of the above study for developing economies, especially India. The present research can be considered as a theoretical guideline for this future research agenda.

Appendix

Derivation of the expressions for $(\hat{X}_A/\hat{K}_F)$, $(\hat{X}_B/\hat{K}_F)$, $(\hat{X}_M/\hat{K}_F)$ and $(\hat{X}_F/\hat{K}_F)$.

Differentiating equation (6) we can get

$$\hat{X}_F = \hat{K}_F \qquad \text{... (10)}$$

Differentiating equation (5) we can get

$$a_{KA}dX_A + a_{KM}dX_M = 0$$

$$\text{or, } \lambda_{KA}\hat{X}_A + \lambda_{KM}\hat{X}_M = 0 \quad \text{... (11)}$$

Differentiating equation (7) we can get

$$a_{LA}dX_A + a_{LB}dX_B + (1+\mu)a_{LM}dX_M + (1+\mu)a_{LF}dX_F = 0$$

$$\text{or, } \lambda_{LA}\hat{X}_A + \lambda_{LB}\hat{X}_B + (1+\mu)\lambda_{LM}\hat{X}_M + (1+\mu)\lambda_{LF}\hat{X}_F = 0$$

Using equation (10), the above equation can be written as

$$\lambda_{LA}\hat{X}_A + \lambda_{LB}\hat{X}_B + (1+\mu)\lambda_{LM}\hat{X}_M = -(1+\mu)\lambda_{LF}\hat{K}_F \quad \text{... (12)}$$

Differentiating equation (9) we can get

$$\lambda_{CA}\hat{X}_A + \lambda_{CB}\hat{X}_B = -f_3(\lambda_{LM}\hat{X}_M + \lambda_{LF}\hat{X}_F)$$

Using equation (10), the above equation can be written as

$$\lambda_{CA}\hat{X}_A + \lambda_{CB}\hat{X}_B + f_3\lambda_{LM}\hat{X}_M = -f_3\lambda_{LF}\hat{K}_F \quad \text{... (13)}$$

From equation (11), (12) and (13) we can write

$$\begin{bmatrix} \lambda_{KA} & 0 & \lambda_{KM} \\ \lambda_{LA} & \lambda_{LB} & (1+\mu)\lambda_{LM} \\ \lambda_{CA} & \lambda_{CB} & f_3\lambda_{LM} \end{bmatrix} = \begin{bmatrix} \hat{X}_A \\ \hat{X}_B \\ \hat{X}_M \end{bmatrix} = \begin{bmatrix} 0 \\ -(1+\mu)\lambda_{LF}\hat{K}_F \\ -f_3\lambda_{LF}\hat{K}_F \end{bmatrix} \quad \text{... (14)}$$

Solving the above by Cramer's rule and simplifying one gets

$$\hat{X}_A = [\lambda_{KM}\{-(1+\mu)\lambda_{CB}\lambda_{LF}\hat{K}_F + f_3\lambda_{LF}\lambda_{LB}\hat{K}_F\}/|\lambda|$$

$$\hat{X}_M = [\lambda_{KA}\{-f_3\lambda_{LB}\lambda_{LF}\hat{K}_F + (1+\mu)\lambda_{LF}\lambda_{CB}\hat{K}_F\}/|\lambda|$$

$$\hat{X}_B = [\lambda_{KM}\{\lambda_{CA}\lambda_{LF}\hat{K}_F - f_3(1+\mu)\lambda_{LF}\lambda_{LA}\hat{K}_F\}/|\lambda| \quad \text{...(15)}$$

$$\text{Where } |\lambda| = \begin{bmatrix} \lambda_{KA} & 0 & \lambda_{KM} \\ \lambda_{LA} & \lambda_{LB} & (1+\mu)\lambda_{LM} \\ \lambda_{CA} & \lambda_{CB} & f_3\lambda_{LM} \end{bmatrix}$$

$$\therefore |\lambda| = [\lambda_{KA}\{f_3\lambda_{LB}\lambda_{LM} - (1+\mu)\lambda_{LM}\lambda_{CB}\}] + [\lambda_{KM}(\lambda_{LA}\lambda_{CB} -$$

$\lambda_{CA}\lambda_{LB})]$ ...(16)

Now $|\lambda|$ is positive under the sufficient condition $f_3 > (1+\mu)(\lambda_{CB}/\lambda_{LB})$ or $f_3 / (\lambda_{CB}/\lambda_{LB}) > (\overline{w}/w)$.

Derivation of the expression for $(\hat{C}/\hat{K}_F)$

Differentiating equation (8) we can get

$$\hat{C} = (L/C)\, f_3\, [-\lambda_{LM}\hat{X}_M - \lambda_{LF}\hat{X}_F]$$

$$\hat{C}/\hat{K}_F = (L/C)\, f_3\, [-\lambda_{LM}(\hat{X}_M/\hat{K}_F) - \lambda_{LF}(\hat{X}_F/\hat{K}_F)]$$

$$\hat{C}/\hat{K}_F = \{f_3(L/C)(\lambda_{LF}\lambda_{KM})(\lambda_{CA}\lambda_{LB} - \lambda_{LA}\lambda_{CB})\}/|\lambda|$$

$\therefore (\hat{C}/\hat{K}_F)$ is negative under the sufficient condition $f_3 > (1+\mu)(\lambda_{CB}/\lambda_{LB}) > (\lambda_{CA}/\lambda_{LA})$. ... (17)

NOTES

1. In these two sectors adult do what children do. Therefore, both types of labour can substitute each other. This assumption of "substitute" is termed as "substitution axioms" by Basu and Van (1998).
2. This assumption is termed as "luxury axiom" by Basu and Van (1998). According to the axiom the workers whose income is close to minimum subsistence level send their children to the job market, so that their income can supplement their low family income. Thus the income earned by the child labourers is some additional amount of income, which their family can use for a little better living. In other words, we can say that the income of child labour is like a luxury item for their family.
3. Owing to the possibility of introduction of the US Arkins Bill, which calls for complete ban on imports of any goods that were manufactured wholly or partly by child workers, the employers in the booming garments industry in Bangladesh that had employed a large number of child workers began removing the child workers drastically. The consequence was a chaotic process that left many children worse off than they had before.
4. For example, family farming by using traditional method of production.

5. Our implicit assumption is that $rF \geq rFw$, where rFw is the exogenously given world rate of return on foreign capital. For this reason foreign capital will be invested in the small open economy but due to government control the amount of foreign capital which enters in this country is also fixed at a particular point of time. It may be noted in this connection that in many developing countries we find that the shift towards more liberalized regime is a gradual one instead of drastic shift. Drastic policy changes may lead socio-political tension in the economy in the short run. The assumption of exogenously given foreign captial stock can thus be justified as the government directly regulates the entry of foreign capital. See Marjit (1994) for details. See also Gupta and Gupta (1998).
6. One can consider for an individual family supply of child labour function as $g(w, wc)$, with $(\partial g/\partial w)<0$ and $(\partial g/\partial\, w\partial)>0$ so that for $(L - aL_{MXM} - a_{LFXF})$ families the total supply of child labour as $C= g(w, w\partial)\ (L - a_{LMXM} - a_{LFXF}) = f\{w, w\partial, (L - a_{LMXM} - a_{LFXF})\}$.
7. Its economic reason has already been mentioned.

REFERENCES

Baland, J. and Robinson, J. A. (2000): 'Is child labour inefficient?'. *Journal of Political Economy,* 108(4), 663-679.

Basu, K. (1999): "Child Labour: Cause, Consequence, and Cure, with Remarks on International Labour Standards", *Journai of Economic Literature,* 37 (September), 1083-1119.

Basu, K. and Van, P.H. (1998): "The Economics of Child Labour", *American Economic Review,* 88(3), 412-427.

Chaudhuri, S. (2000): "Incidence of Child Labour, Free Education Policy and Trade Liberalization in a Small Open Economy: A Theoretical analysis", *mimeo,* Department of Economics, University of Calcutta.

Chaudhuri, S. and Dwibedi, J.K. (2006): "Foreign Capital Inflow, Education Subsidy and Incidence of Child Labour in a Developing Economy", *mimeo,* Department of Economics, University of Calcutta.

Chaudhuri, S. and Gupta, M.R. (2004): "Child labour and Trade Liberalization", *Japanese Economic Review,* 55(2), 201-211.

Cigno, A., Rosati, F. C. and Guarcello, L. (2002): 'Does globalization increase child labour?', *World Development,* 30(9), 1579-1589.

Dessy, S.E. (2000): "A Defense of Compulsive Measures Against Child Labour", *Journal of Development Economics,* 62: 261-275.

Dwibedi, J. and Chaudhuri, S. (2003): "Trade Liberalization, Foreign Capital Inflow and Incidence of Child Labour in a Developing Economy", *mimeo,* Department of Economics, University of Calcutta.

Edmonds, E.V. (2002): "Reduziert die Globalisierung die Kinderarbeit?", *Neue Zurcher Zeitung*, February 23/24: p. 29.

Eswaran, M. (1996): "Fertility, Literacy, and the Institution of Child Labour", *CRESP Discussion Paper:* DP No. 36, The University of British Columbia.

Grootaert, C. (1998): "Child labour in Cote d'Ivoire: Incidence and Determinants", in "The Policy Analysis of Child Labour: A Comparative Study", C. Grootaert and H. Patrinos (eds), *manuscript, World Bank,* Washington.

Harris, J.R. and M.P. Todaro (1970): "Migration, Unemployment and Development: A Two Sector Analysis", *American Economic Review,* 60:126-142.

Jafarey, S. and Lahiri, S. (2002): "Will trade sanctions reduce child labour? The role of credit markets", *Journal of Development Economics,* 68(1), 137-156.

Ranjan, P. (2001): "Credit constraints and the phenomenon of child labour", *Journal of Development Economics,* 64, 81-102.

Swaminathan, M. (1998): "Economic Growth and the Persistence of Child Labour: Evidence from an Indian City", *World Development,* 26(8), 1513-1528.

5

Liberalization, Competition and Capacity Utilization in Indian Iron and Steel Industry

Sarbapriya Ray and *Mihir Kumar Pal*

1. Introduction

Since 1991, a series of market-based reforms have been initiated by Government of India, which has supposed to bring about significant changes in industrial sectors. As a result, Indian industries have been witnessing profound changes in the basic parameters governing its structure and functioning. Relaxing of licensing rule, reduction in tariff rates, removal of restriction on import of raw materials and technology, price decontrol, rationalization of customs and excise duty, enhancement of the limit of foreign equity participation etc. are among those which have been introduced at early 1990s. The major objectives of such policy reforms were to make Indian industries as well as entire economy more efficient, technologically up-to-date, competitive and ready to face global challenges with a view of attain rapid growth. It was obviously expected that liberalization would enhance competition and at the same time, this would increase the competitiveness of the domestic firms so that they can thrive despite facing global pressure of competition. A significant improvement in industrial production began since 1993 with the liberalization policy becoming effective with industrial delicensing. Easy availability of imported inputs eliminated the difference between actual and potential productive capacity. The advocates of liberalization believe that this policy reform will improve industrial growth and performance significantly while critics argue that total withdrawal of restrictions on several matters will have a negative effect on future growth and performance of the industry.

As a part and parcel of self-appraisal, each and every industry is constantly engaged in search of tools for assessing its own current performance. This performance can be judged suitably by comparing it with the various targets, past achievements and operative capacity. Business decision-making and policy formulation mostly depend on economic indicators. In a capital scare economy like India, manufacturing capacity utilization is such a key indicator of economic performance which not only determines how much more output can be obtained by fuller utilization of existing capacity but also defines the required expansion of capacity for a targeted output and also explains changes in investment, inflation, level of resource utilization etc.

In this perspective, this analytical study strives to gauge the performance of Indian Iron and Steel Industry in the light of capacity utilization. This paper also examines the impact of liberalization on capacity utilization and assesses whether reforms in industrial sector have made the Indian Iron and Steel Industry more competitive or not and also the pace of competition within the industry has been tried to evaluate. It is necessary to acknowledge that CU in not the only parameter in measuring performance of an industry where there exists profitability and productivity variables in performance evaluation.

The Plan of the Paper is as follows:

Section 2 depicts conceptual issues related to capacity. Section 3 provides database and methodology. Section 4 estimates capacity and its utilization and also assesses the impact of liberalization on capacity utilization. Section 5 critically analyses the nature of competition in the liberalized regime. Section 6 presents threats of liberalization and policy measures to be adopted for the survival of the said industry and Section 7 presents summary and conclusions.

2. Brief Review of Literature on Concept of Capacity

Capacity utilization is an economic concept which refers to the extent to which an enterprise or a nation actually uses its installed productive capacity. Thus, it refers to the relationship between actual output produced and potential output that could be produced with installed equipment, if capacity was fully used. Capacity utilization measures as a procyclical indicator have been widely used to explain economic fluctuations. Unlike many well defined concepts, capacity has been subjected to alternative definition and misconceptions.

Engineer's idea of capacity may differ from economist's idea because if certain volume of production is technically possible, it may not be economically desirable. One of the most used definitions of CU rate is as the ratio of actual output to potential output. Concerning the potential output, there are several ways to define it. One is the engineering or technical approach according to which potential output represents the maximum amount of output that can be produced in the short run with existing stock of capital (see Nelson, 1989: 273). A similar discussion can be found in Johansen (1968) [see Fare, Grosskopf and Kokkelenberg, 1989: 655] where the author defines the capacity as being "…. the maximum amount that can be produced per unit of time with existing plant and equipment, provided that the availability of variable factors of production is not restricted". Following the last definition, in one of his papers, Fare (1994) describes the necessary and sufficient conditions for the existence of plant capacity as defined by Johansen. In a similar fashion, Fare, Grosskopf and Kokkelenberg (1989) developed measures of plant capacity, plant capacity utilization and technical change in the short run for multi-product firms, based on frontier models using non-parametric linear programming method (DEA).

But, operating manager's notion of installed capacity may differ which assumes a variety of considerations such as number of shifts in work, quality of managerial staff, and availability of repair and replacement parts all of which suppose to modify the engineering estimation of plant capacity. Concept of installed capacity particularly is linked to the shift work decision problem which associates the problem of selecting an optimal number of shifts of work—single, double or triple shift. If a firm desires to operate on a single shift basis, the capacity output can be based on this assumption and it would be possible to have 100 per cent capacity utilization rate if time utilization rate of capital is nearly 33 per cent (as because firms operates on a single shift basis of eight hours for each shift assuming that there exists maximum three shifts). Whether decision of capital expansion or multi-shift operation will be undertaken depend, by and large, on the matter of weighing the alternative costs and gains both in short-run and long-run. Between two alternatives—expansion of new plant facilities or moving towards multi-shift operation, it is inevitable that most of the developing countries like India would favour the use of multi-shift operation in comparison with the further expansion of investment project because if customers' demand is rising gradually and new equipment is not available or is costly to replace, multi-shift operation would save additional capital outlay and at the same time generates employment opportunities without involving additional capital expenditure. It is also true that where there is underutilization of capacity, there is ample scope of utilizing capital more extensively by increasing working shifts in the industry. Nevertheless, a major lacuna in this engineering approach is that it does not explain the variations in capacity utilization mainly due to lack of any economic foundation.

The economic approach, on the other hand, defines the potential output as being the optimum level of output from the economic point of view. This alternative considers capital as a quasi fixed input and allows for distinction between short and long run cost curves. In the long run, capital can be adjusted in order to achieve optimal (cost minimizing/profit maximizing) level. In the short run, capital is fixed and only the variable inputs can be varied. The short run equilibrium output, for a competitive firm, is then given by the equality between exogenous output price and the Short Run Marginal Cost curve (SRMC), Y^*. The potential output would then correspond to that level of output at which Short Run Average Total Cost (SRATC) is minimized-Y^{**}(and equal to Long Run Average Total Cost, LRATC).

The definition of output as Y^{**} corresponds to the cost-minimization problem while Y^* corresponds to the profit-maximization. As pointed out in Berndt, Hesse and Morrison (1981), this difference can affect short run equilibrium in the sense that it may or may not occur at the level of output were the SRATC reaches its minimum: $Y^* > Y^{**}$ OR ($Y^* < Y^{**}$) when the output price is greater than (lower than) the minimum level of SRATC. The author's address also the issue of how variations in input prices might affect the minimum point of the SRATC and hence Y^{**}.

The economic approach was first analyzed by Cassel (1937) and later on, two more definitions have been introduced. The first was suggested by Klein (1960) and Friedman (1963) and recently Segerson and Squires (1990), who define the potential output as being the output level at which the long run and short run average total cost curves are tangent. Klein (1960) argued that long run average cost curve may not have a minimum and proposed the output level where the short run average cost curve is tangent to the long run average cost curve as an alternative measure of capacity output.

The second approach supported by Cassel (1937) and Hickman (1964) takes as reference the output level at which the short run average total cost curve reaches its minimum. Therefore, an economically more meaningful definition of capacity output originated by Cassel (1937) is the level of production where the firm's long run average cost curve reaches a minimum. As we consider the long run average cost, no input is held fixed. For a firm with the typical 'U' shaped average cost curve, at this capacity level of output, economies of scale have been exhausted.but diseconomies have not set in. The physical limit defines the capacity of one or more quasi-fixed input. Klein defined capacity as the maximum sustainable level of output an industry can attain within a very short time, when not constrained by the demand for product and the industry is operating its existing stock of capital at its customary level of intensity.

Hickman (1964) suggests that capacity is defined as that output which can be produced at minimum average total cost, given the existing stock of plant and equipment and existing techniques and factor prices. The level of capacity is inferred from observed investment behaviour. Regression methods are used to estimate a relationship between desired capital stock and several explanatory variables including output, relative prices and time, on the hypothesis that net investment occurs in proportion to the excess of desired over actual stock. The relationship between desired capital stock and output is then inverted to yield a corresponding relationship between capacity and actual capital stock for given prices and techniques. The method is used to calculate aggregate capacity annually for 1949-1960 and the properties of the resulting estimates are discussed. New estimates of capacity and its utilization in manufacturing are also presented and compared with those of other investigators.

The relationship between the two economic measures of Capacity Utilization (CU) depends on the degree of scale economics for the unit that is being analyzed. Berndt and Hesse (1986) advocate that under the assumption of prevailing constant return to scale in the long run, the tangency point between the long run and short run curves will coincide with the point where the long run and short run average total cost curve reach their minimum. Hence, two economic measures of CU would be equivalent. Nelson (1989) argued that Capacity Utilization (CU) is usually defined as the ratio of actual output to the output corresponding to (i) the minimum point on the SRATC curve, (ii) the point of tangency between the LRATC and SRATC curves. In practice, however, CU is often measured as the ratio of actual to the maximum potential output consistent with a given capital stock. This paper demonstrates how to estimate the theoretical measures of CU, and examines the correlation between the three measures of CU, and the McGraw-Hill estimates of CU, using data from a sample of US privately owned electric utilities for 1961-1983. Nelson (1989, p: 274), using data from a sample of US privately owned electric utilities reaches the conclusion that: 'The choice of a particular measure of CU may be little consequence if all of the measures are highly correlated, and if the correlation is constant over time and across firms. If this is not the case, however, the choice may influence the conclusions to be drawn from a study."

Questions about the definition and construction of capacity utilization measure are often based on distinctions between "engineering" or "technical" as compared to "economic" measures, "maximum" *versus* "optimal" usage of capacity, and "primal" as contrasted to "dual" representations of the notion of "best", or optimum. The many combinations and permutations of these concepts offered in the literature often differ in terms of the definition and treatment of the stocks defining the capacity base, and the variable inputs determining their utilization. The basic conceptual issue is that engineering or technical measures represent the most output that can physically be produced given the existing input base, whereas one might think a policy-relevant measure of potential output should instead be founded on some notion of (economic) "optimization" rather than (physical) "maximization". By contrast, economic measures are founded on the idea of an optimum amount of output that might be produced, in terms of the costs or profits emanating from production. This alternative perspective can be represented by a dual cost (or profit) function, defined in terms of the minimum possible input costs required to produce a given amount of output, taking both technological and behavioural optimization into account. We prefer choice theoretic model (Cassel's model) because it is firmly based on the behavioural concept of economic theory.

Data Base and Methodology

Study Period

This study covers a period of 25 years from 1979-80 to 2003-04. For our analytical purpose, the study period chosen was from 1979-80 to 2003-04. This was partly because: though Indian economy was liberalized in 1991, with some tentativeness, it has been opened to the world economy during mid-eighties and partly because of the non-availability of all types of data required for our study before 1979-80. The entire period is divided into two phases as pre-reform period (1979-80 to 1991-92) and post-reform period (1991-92 to 2003-04), sub-division of period being taken logically as such to assess conveniently the impact of liberalization on TFPG and CU. Selection of time period is largely guided by availability of data.[1]

Description of Data and Variables

Difficulty faced by researchers in conducting studies on CU in Indian industries is that available official data on Industrial capacities are quite unsatisfactory. The present study is based on industry-level time series data as well as firm-level panel data taken from several issues of ASI, National Accounts Statistics (NAS), Centre for Monitoring Indian Economy (CMIE), Economic Survey, Statistical Abstract (several issues), RBI bulletin on Currency and Finance etc. covering a period of 25 years commencing from 1979-80 to 2003-04. Selection of time period is largely guided by availability of data.

Output and Variable Cost

Output is measured as real value added produced by manufacturers which is the sum of labour, capital and energy costs. It is symbolically defined as ($Y = P_L L + P_K.K_{-1} + P_E.E$) which is suitably deflated by Wholesale Index of Prices (WIP) index for manufactured product (base 1981-82 = 100). The data for wholesale index of prices have been collected from Statistical Abstract (several issues). Deflation has been done to offset the influence of price changes. L, K and E are the labour, capital and energy input respectively and P_L, P_K, P_E etc. are their respective prices.

Labour and Price of Labour

In the context of developing economy like India, in all major works on the manufacturing sectors conducted by Goldar (1986), Ahluwalia (1991), Balakrishnan and Pushpangadan (1994), Das, Debkusum (2004), they consider 'total employees' as the measure of labour input. The logic behind this is that there exists an imperfection in the labour market and inappropriateness of the assumption of efficiency of different categories of labour being reflected in their rates of remuneration in the Indian context.

Following the same line as applicable to Indian economy, total number of persons engaged in respective industrial sector is used as a measure of labour inputs. Price of labour (P_L) is the total emolument (total wage payment as available in Annual Survey of Industries) divided by number of labourers which includes both production and non-production workers like administrative, technical and clerical staff (Goldar *et al.*, 2004). In recent issues of Annual Survey of Industries (ASI), it is reported under the head 'persons engaged', while for earlier issues, it is reported as 'number of employees'. 'Total employees' as a measure of labour input includes both workers and persons other than workers. The latter category of employees, i.e. 'persons other than employees' includes supervisors, technicians, managers, clerks and other similar types of employees. But, one serious limitation of this assumption is that this does not take into account variations in quality and the composition of labour force. Nevertheless, we are compelled to consider 'persons engaged' as labour input owing to data limitation.

Energy and Price Energy

Deflated cost of fuel (Appendix-A1) has been taken as measure of energy inputs. Due to unavailability of data regarding periodic price series of energy in India, some approximation become necessary. We have taken weighted aggregative average price index of fuel (considering coal, petroleum and electricity price index, suitably weighted, from statistical abstract) as proxy price of energy.[3]

Capital Stock and Price of Capital

Deflated gross fixed capital stock at 1981-82 prices is taken as the measure of capital input. The estimates are based on perpetual inventory method (Appendix-A2). Rental price of capital is assumed to be the price of capital (P_K) which can be estimated following Jorgenson and Griliches (1967):

$$P^t_K = r_t + d_t - \frac{P^*_K}{P_K}$$

Where r_t is the rate of return on capital in year t, d_t is the rate of depreciation of capital in the year *t* and $\frac{P^*_K}{P_K}$ is the rate of appreciation of capital. Rate of return is taken as the rate of interest on long term government bonds and securities[4] which is collected from RBI bulletin (various issues). The rate of depreciation is estimated from the reported figures on depreciation and fixed capital as available in ASI which Murty (1986) had done earlier. However, we have not tried corrections for the appreciation of value of capital[5] in the estimates of price of capital services.

The variables are depicted below in Table 1 in a nut shell.

Table 1: Description of variables for calculating CU levels

Variable	*Description*	*Nature in production process*
Output:	Deflated real value added	—
Inputs:		
Labour	Total persons engaged (Production workers+ non-production workers)	Variable
Energy	Deflated cost of fuel	Variable
Capital	Real gross fixed capital stock (*t*) = real gross fixed capital stock (*t* – 1) + real gross investment (*t*).	Quasi-fixed

Model for Capacity Utilization

The choice theoretic approach defines capacity output as the long run desired level of output given capital stock and input prices. A firm faced with adjustment costs for capital may choose to operate in the short run at a level of output that differs from long run desired level. Variations in capacity utilization are viewed as a short run phenomenon caused by quasi-fixed nature of capital. The recent development of econometrically tractable short run variable cost functions that incorporate capital as a quasi-fixed input has permitted researchers to estimate *CU* within a choice theoretic framework.

Economic capacity is a short run concept. The fixed nature of some inputs like capital characterizes short run. For any amount of fixed input like capital, the output which can be obtained with the minimum long run cost method is capacity output which will require a higher cost method of production and therefore, short run average cost of output is above the long run average cost curve except at the capacity output level. In the short run, higher cost methods are required to obtain additional output since only variable inputs may be increased. Therefore, a firm with fixed capital may choose to operate in the short run at a level of output that differs from the long run desired level and variation in CU is viewed as a short run phenomenon due to quasi-fixity of capital.

Considering variations in *CU* as a short-run phenomenon caused by the quasi-fixed nature of capital, an econometrically tractable short-run variable-cost function which assumes capital as a quasi-fixed input has been used in our study to estimate *CU*.

We consider a single output and three input framework (K, L, E) in estimating CU and assume that firms produce output within the technological constraint of a well-behaved production function. A production function is considered to be well-behaved if it has positive marginal product for each input and it is quasi-concave and also satisfies the conditions of monotonocity. Quasi-concavity required that the bordered Hessian matrix of first and second partial derivatives of the production function be negative semi-definite.

However, in our study, $Y = f(K, L, E)$ where K, L and E are capital, labour and energy respectively. Since capacity output is a short run notion, the basic concept behind it is that firm faces short run constraints like stock of capital. Firms operate at full capacity where their existing capital stock is at long run optimal level. Capacity output is that level of output which would make existing short run capital stock optimal.

Rate of *CU* is given as:

$$CU = Y/Y^* \qquad \text{... (1)}$$

Y is actual output and Y^* is capacity output.

In association with variable profit function, there exist a variable -cost function which can be expressed as

$$VC = f(P_L, P_E, K, Y) \quad \text{... (2)}$$

Short run total cost function is expressed as

$$\text{STC} = \text{f}(P_L, P_E, K, Y) + P_K K \quad \text{... (3)}$$

P_K is the rental price of Capital.

Variable cost equation which is variant of general quadratic form for (2) that provide a closed form expression for Y^* is specified as

$$VC = \alpha_o + K_{-1}\left(\alpha_k + \tfrac{1}{2}\beta_{KK}\left[\frac{K-1}{Y}\right] + \beta_{KL.}P_L + \beta_{KE.}P_E\right)$$

$$+ P_L\left(\alpha_L + \tfrac{1}{2}\beta_{LL.}P_L + \beta_{LE.}P_E + \beta_{LY.}Y\right)$$

$$+ P_E\left(\alpha_E + \tfrac{1}{2}\beta_{EE.}P_E + \beta_{EY.}Y +\right) + Y\left(a_Y + \tfrac{1}{2}\beta_{YY.}Y\right) \quad \text{... (4)}$$

Similar functional form has been previously estimated by Denny *et al.* (1981). The variable cost function is based on the assumption that some input like capital cannot be adjusted to their equilibrium level. Therefore, the firm minimizes variable cost given the output and the quasi-fixed inputs like capital.

Here, K_{-1} is the capital stock at the beginning of the year which implies that a firm makes output decisions constrained by the capital stock at the beginning of the year.

Capacity output (Y*) for a given level of quasi-fixed factor is defined as that level of output which minimizes STC. So, the optimal capacity output level, for a given level of quasi-fixed factors, is defined as that level of output which minimizes STC. So, at the optimal capacity output level, the envelop theorem implies that the following relation must exist.

$$\partial STC / \partial K = \partial VC / \partial K + P_K = 0 \quad \text{... (5)}$$

In estimating Y^*, we differentiate VC equation (4) w.r.t K_{-1} and substitute expression in equation (5)

$$Y^* = \frac{-\beta_{KK} . K_{-1}}{(\alpha_K + \beta_{KL}P_L + \beta_{KE}P_E + P_K)} \quad \text{... (6) and (1)}$$

The estimates of CU can be obtained by combining equation (6) and (1).

Analysis of Capacity and its Utilization

In this section, analysis of the results regarding measurement and trend in capacity utilization of glass sector in India under our consideration is presented. In order to facilitate comparison of the estimates, we have also subdivided the entire period into 1979-80 to 1991-92 which is termed as pre-reform period and 1991-92 to 2003-04 as post-reform period. Before presenting the result, descriptive statistics showing the differences in the statistics for the variables under consideration for the two time periods are depicted in the following Table 2. The descriptive table indicates that mean and standard deviation of all variables have been enhanced significantly during post reform periods.

At first hand, the result section depicts the results of a multiple regression analysis applied to measure capacity output and the trend in capacity utilization. The variable cost equation shown as equation (4) has been estimated by the Ordinary Least Square methods (OLS). Our model assumes that capacity Utilization (*CU*) is a function of input prices, output and quasi-fixed capital. We find that Capacity Utilization and input prices have a negative relationship and capacity utilization (*CU*) and output have a positive one. The derivative of *VC* (equation 4) with respect to *K* is negative since capital will substitute labour and energy. In order to test for the concavity of the variable cost function with respect to variable input prices, its Hessian matrix for negative semi-definiteness is evaluated and it is found that concavity condition is fulfilled at all observation points. Therefore, the partial derivative with respect to each of input prices is negative. The partial derivative of *VC* with respect to output is positive because in our empirical results, $B_{KK} > 0$ and $(B_{KL}P_L + B_{KE}P_E + P_K) < 0$ for all data points. Therefore, positive relation between output and Capacity Utilization (*CU*) is an indication that an increase in demand will lead to higher levels of capacity utilization.

First, it emerges from the estimated results that CU ratios are less than unity for all observations. There is a prominent diminishing trend in capacity utilization over years because average CU declined from 0.7781 in pre-reform period to 0.7212 in post-reform period implying a decline of 7.31 per cent as well as same declining trend

Table 2: Descriptive Statistics

Variables	*Pre- reform period*				*Post-reform period*			
	Minimum	*Maximum*	*Mean*	*Standard deviation*	*Minimum*	*Maximum*	*Mean*	*Standard deviation*
Variable cost (Rs. crore)	1102	2355	1585.31	106.33	1864	7600	4948.58	432.78
Output (Rs. crore)	1530	3651	2615.23	195.08	3595	11046	8110.67	698.32
Capital (Rs. crore)	12939	26197	18118	1110.48	26197	47492	37469.92	2077.08
Energy price (Rs.)	0.6853	2.345	1.51	0.1463	2.78	7.41	4.76	0.4345
Labour price (Rs.)	0.001286	0.003632	0.002322	0.00022	0.004689	0.015	0.0092	0.00093
Price of capital (Rs.)	0.1092	0.2034	0.1547	0.0099	0.1316	0.2105	0.1761	0.00597
Total observations	13				12			

The following table displays vivid portrait regarding variation in capacity utilization. The following key observations can be found out.

Table 3: Capacity utilization of Iron and Steel Industry in India at aggregate level, 1979-80 to 2003-04.

Pre-reform period (1979-80 to 1991-92)							*Post-reform period (1991-92 to 2003-04)*						
Year	*Actual output (Cr. Rs)*	*Capacity output (Cr.Rs)*	*CU*	*Output growth*	*Capacity growth*	*Growth rate of CU*	*Year*	*Actual output*	*Capacity output*	*CU*	*Output growth*	*Capacity growth*	*Growth rate of CU*
79-80	1548	2453	0.6311	—	—	—	91-92	3595	4056	0.8863	-1.53	—	23.38
80-81	1530	2529	0.6050	-1.16	3.10	-0.159	92-93	4681	5570	0.8404	30.21	37.33	-8.94
81-82	1901	2543	0.7475	24.25	0.55	21.22	93-94	4902	5536	0.8854	4.72	-0.6104	6.73
82-83	2349	2720	0.8668	23.56	6.96	16.25	94 - 95	5177	7402	0.6994	5.61	33.71	-21.25
83-84	2313	3003	0.7702	-1.53	10.40	-10.13	95-96	6427	12447	0.5163	24.15	68.16	-25.97
84-85	2683	3215	0.8345	16.00	7.06	6.70	96 –97	7139	13484	0.5294	11.08	8.33	13.61
85-86	2487	3317	0.7498	-7.31	3.17	-5.96	97– 98	8321	11314	0.7355	16.56	-16.09	30.62
86-87	2646	3314	0.7984	6.39	-0.09	6.012	98– 99	8266	9750	0.8478	-0.6609	-13.82	-2.42
87-88	2880	3598	0.8004	8.84	8.57	-0.055	99– 00	9378	11162	0.8402	13.45	14.48	20.16
88-89	2961	3892	0.7608	2.81	8.17	-5.84	00– 01	10435	19623	0.5318	11.27	75.8	-36.49
89-90	3454	4231	0.8163	16.65	8.71	7.39	01– 02	10821	12097	0.8945	3.70	-38.35	66.29
90-91	3651	4306	0.8479	5.70	1.77	-12.69	02 - 03	11046	16221	0.6809	2.079	34.09	-22.73
91-92	3595	4056	0.8863	-1.53	-6.16	23.38	03 –04	10735	22100	0.4881	-2.82	36.24	-28.34
average			0.7781	7.13	4.02	3.54				0.7212	9.06	18.40	1.13

Source: Own estimate.

was set in average growth rate of *CU* (as is evident from Table 3). This implies that actual output fell far short of capacity output of Indian Iron and Steel Industry which in turn signifies a widening difference between capacity output and actual output. Trend in capacity utilization indicates the presence of idle or excess capacity in the industry for the entire study period.

Second, if capacity output is taken to be the economic capacity derived from optimization process, the *CU* ratio could exceed one or it may be less than one. The implication of economic *CU* less than unity (as our result suggests) is that production is to the left of the minimum point of short run average total cost curve which further signifies that Indian steel sector could have reduced its short run generation costs with gradually moving to the tangency point or minimum point of the short run average cost curve.

Third, it is apparent from our study that the economic *CU* index ranges from about 0.4881 to 0.8863. Capacity expansion varies from 4.02 per cent to 18.4 per cent during these two time frames. Moreover, the correlation between actual output (*Q*) and capacity output (*CQ*) is quite high over the entire time period which is nearly 0.9352.

Fourth, a comparison of the average utilization of capacity in the two periods (Table 3 above) showed a slightly lower average utilization in the post-reform period as compared to pre-reform period. The *CU* trends have also registered a gradual decline since mid- nineties. Increasing trends have been noticed in the average growth rate of capacity output and actual output during those two periods. During pre-reform period, capacity expansion was not improved rapidly probably due to licensing restriction but abolition of license-raj during post-reform period paved the way for drastic expansion of capacity. Although it is true that there is no precise way of distinguishing the various factors that contributed to declining utilization rate, a shift from a restrictive trade regime to a more liberalized trade perhaps decelerates the utilization rate because it might be mainly due to gradually rapid and abrupt expansion of capacity but comparatively slow improvement in the growth rate of actual output as well as actual demand. Capacity has been expanded rapidly because licensing requirement for capacity creation has been abolished coupled with private players being came into operation for creation of additional capacity. The slower growth rate of actual output in steel industry in India particularly might be due to the fact that there exists excess supply situation resulted either by huge imported steel from China, Ukraine etc. or by entry of foreign private players capturing a substantial portion of domestic market shares coupled with massive investment made earlier in the Greenfield Steel Projects in India by the private players with the expectation of enormous prospective earnings from the project despite well known global excess capacity.

Trends growth rate of capacity utilization of Indian Iron and Steel Industry at aggregate level are presented in Table 4 to support the above-mentioned result. The semi-log function was finally selected to explain the trend. The semi-log model is log $Y = a + bt$, where Y = Capacity utilization, a = Constant, t = Time in years, b = Regression coefficient and in this model, the growth rate will be ($b \times 100$) in terms of percentage.

Table 4: Trend Growth rate of capacity, output and capacity utilization

Pre-reform period (1979-80 to 1991-92)				*Post- reform period (1991-92 to 2003-04)*			
Indus-try/year	*Capacity*	*Output*	*Capacity utili-zation*	*Indus-try/year*	*Cap-acity*	*Output*	*Capa-city utili-zation*
Iron and steel	2.19* (16.61)#	3.08 (11.54)	0.8874 (3.25)	Iron and steel	5.02 (6.32)	4.06 (13.41)	-0.947 (-2.29)
Adjusted R^2	0.69	0.89	0.49		0.78	0.94	0.13

* trend growth rate,

\# t values.

Source: Estimated from semi-log trend

Estimated result in Table 4 supports the contention that capacity grows rapidly in post-reform period, simultaneously output growth declined. This results in declining growth rate in capacity utilization. It is expected that no single explanation for variations in capacity utilization in this industry group will hold true. Nevertheless, it seems that due to heavy investment in the 1990s, unaccompanied by commensurate expansion of demand, capacity utilization went on worsening in this manufacturing industry.

Table 5 presents studies of Indian manufacturing since 2003 with area of study, input, output, functional forms, and results. The present study differs from previous studies in several ways. This is the only comprehensive study on Iron and Steel Industry during the last three decades, especially during post-reform period after 1991. This is the first study of capacity utilization using variant of quadratic cost function on Indian Iron and Steel Industry. All but two studies uses data which are over a decade old and four studies employed translog cost function. Results of capacity utilization on steel sector in India are comparable to other studies. Majority of Indian studies on capacity utilization shows declining growth rate of capacity utilization during 1990s after economic liberalization took place which are similar to our study.

Impact of Liberalization on Economic CU

In investigating the issue of whether there exists any positive or negative impact of economic reforms on *CU*, dummy variables are used to allow both the intercept and the slope to be different after 1991 onward. Thus, we estimate a typical regression equation

$$L_n Y = A + A'D + Bt + B'D_t$$

Where D is the dummy variable with value equal to zero for the years up to 1990-91 and one thereafter and *Y* is the capacity utilization ratio. The co-efficient of multiplicative dummy term, '*B*', if it positive or negative and significant, will show that there was favourable or adverse impact of economic reform on capacity utilization in the post-reform period. The result of the regression is following:

$$L_n Y = -0.4412 + 0.348D + 0.017t - 0.03295D_t$$
$$(-4.20)\ (2.31)\ (1.21)\ (-1.98)$$

$$R^2 = 0.25$$

Figure in the brackets are *t*-values. As the multiplicative dummy is negative and significant at five per cent level, we can conclude that economic reforms have adverse impact on capacity utilization in the post-reforms period.

Table 5: Capacity utilization results of some previous Indian studies

Year	*author*	*Study area*	*Data*	*Function*	*Functional form*	*Inputs*	*Technology*	*Result*
2003	Danish, A. Hashim	Indian airlines	1964-65 to 1999-2000	cost	translog	Labour, capital, energy/material	Time trend	Declining growth rate
2005	Abdul Azeez Erumban	Indian Manufacturing	1974-2000	cost	translog	Labour, capital, fuel, material	Time trend	Cyclical pattern of growth
2007	Kaustuva Barik	Indian Paper Industry	1973-74 to 1997-98	cost	translog	Labour, capital, energy, non-energy raw material	Time trend	Declining growth rate
2007	Gajanan and Malhotra	Indian Manufacturing	1976-1996	cost	generalized Leontief	Labour, capital	Time trend	CU dropped in the mid-80s, rising again in the early 90s
2008	Goldar and Renganathan	Indian Manufacturing	1996-2003	cost	translog	Labour, capital, energy, material	Time trend	CU fell in1995-01, rose in 2001-04
2009	Kumar and Arora	Indian Sugar Industry	1974-75 to 2004-05	Production	DEA Non-parametric frontier	Labour, capital, intermediate inputs	Time trend	Steep declining growth rate

Now, to understand the impact of liberalization on capacity utilization more precisely, we use a piecewise linear regression equation (popularly known as Spline function) where it is assumed that capacity utilization increases linearly with the passage of time until the threshold time period (t_0)[Here, t_0=1990-91 being last year of pre-reform period after which post-liberalization era begins] after which also it changes linearly with the passage of time but at a much steeper rate. Therefore, we have a piece-wise linear regression consisting of two linear pieces or segments. The CU function changes its slope at the threshold value (t_0=12). Given the data on *CU*, time period and the value of threshold level, the technique of dummy variables can be used to estimate the slopes of the two segments of the piece-wise linear regression. The piecewise linear regression equation is as follows:

$$l_n Z_t = A + Bt + B'(t - t_0) D_t$$

Result of the regression equation is as follows:-

$$l_n Z_t = -0.4289 + 0.01417t - 0.033D_t$$

(-4.43) (2.24) (-1.98)

$R^2 = 0.26$

Figures in the parentheses are the absolute values of t statistics and R^2 is the goodness of fit. Here B gives the slope of the regression line in pre-reform period which is positive and significant at 5 per cent level. This implies that growth in *CU* shows positive trend immediately before liberalization starts.

Co-efficient of the difference between two time period is significant at 5 per cent level and negative (coefficient being -0.033), conclusive inference can be drawn in that liberalization has its significant adverse impact on capacity utilization during post- reforms period.

It is visible from the estimated average growth rate in CU as shown in table 3 that there is a significant decline in average growth rate of *CU* from 3.54 per cent in pre-reform period to 1.13 per cent in post-reform period.

A firm's competitive position in the industry is ascertained by its ability of retaining or enhancing market share by any means. The process of deregulation and liberalization has increased the intensity of competition in iron and steel sector. These changes have led to the restructuring of this industrial sector. The restructuring has affected output growth as well as capacity utilization in negative direction in Indian Iron and Steel Industry from 1991-92 to 2003-04. Berndt and Fuss (1986) and Morrison (1988) show that there lies a systematic relationship between capital-to-output ratio and CU. This relationship becomes operational through Tobin's *q*.[6] If $B_{KK} > 0$, then a rise in capital-to-output ratio will lower Tobin's q and hence will lower *CU* rates. Since in our estimates, $B_{KK} > 0$ for all data points, industries with high capital-output ratios will have lower level of *CU* assuming that other things remain the same. This induce us to infer that the Iron and Steel Industry whose industrial structures depends heavily on traditional manufacturing activities and have higher capital-to-output ratios will generally tend to have lower rates of *CU*. Furthermore, it is noticed from our results that *CU* is more sensitive to the extent of capital deepening of the steel sector. *CU* is regressed on K_{-1}/Y and Y (*GVA*) and the relationship was as follows:

$$CU = 1.33 - 0.0734\, K_{-1}/Y - 0.00003Y$$

$$(3.85)\ (-1.99)\ (-1.76)$$

$$R^2 = 0.16$$

Our result suggests a negative and statistically significant association between *CU* and K_{-1}/Y which implies that the low CU rate is correlated with high capital-to-output ratio and *vice versa* and association between *CU* and *Y* is found to be statistically insignificant.

5. Competition

Liberalization of economy in 1991 has resulted in important changes in business surroundings in which companies are operated resulting in an increase in competition. A scenario of decreasing competition or increasing protection does not exert competitive pressure on domestic industry mainly on account of the moderate effect of protection. Increasing competition exerts pressure on prices and availability of goods and consequently on corporate bottom lines. It is important to assess whether competition in the Iron and Steel Industry has increased over the post-liberalization time period or not.

The Porter model has been adopted here in the context of broad policy changes that has taken place in Indian industry during post-reform period.

(1) Licensing of capacities has been withdrawn in almost all the sectors. This allowed producers in quite a lot of key sectors to expand capacities and set up big plants. Economies of scale resulting from such expansion led to improvement in cost efficiencies.

Import duties on capital goods have been brought down drastically. This reduced cost of new projects in line with those prevalent in developed countries.

Several sectors (like cement and coal) in which government had complete control on distribution and pricing were partially or completely decontrolled.

Restrictions on foreign participation in joint venture (i.e. in commercial vehicles) were relaxed leading to greater transfer of technological know-how.

These changes have certainly reduced protection and at the same time improved linkage between the domestic and international industry. The diminution in import duties has also led to a decline in the cost of key raw materials and accelerated imports. Changes in the degree of competition against the backdrop of these broad policy changes are analyzed in the present part of this paper.

Porter Model: The Porter model focuses on four main factors: (1) Buyers power, (2) Suppliers power, (3) Entry barrier, (4) Threat of substitutes.

Chart 1: Porter model

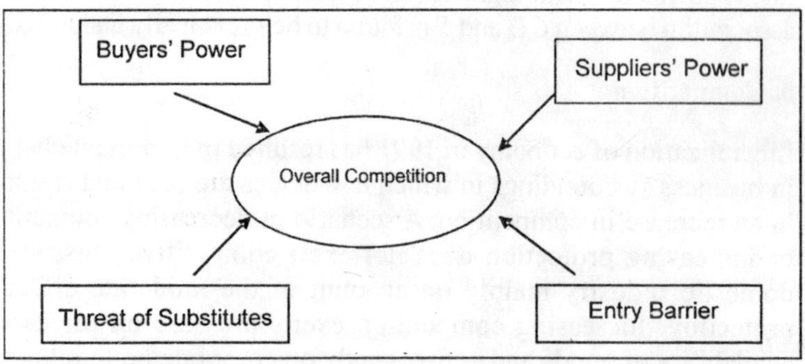

Buyers' Power

Competition in an industry increases if buyers' power increase and *vice versa* . Buyers' power is high in industries where monopsony (large number of sellers and limited number of buyers) exists.

Typically, buyers' power is high in industries where government is the sole buyer of goods, i.e. in industry related to defense machinery.

Rising level of private participation in industry (mainly due to delicensing of capacities in most manufacturing sectors) has led to a wider base of customers in post-liberalization period. This has induced a decline in buyers power for manufacturers in steel industry. A decline in buyers power has reduced competition, but increasing availability of substitutes and greater quality requirements of customers has offset this reduction. Therefore, buyers' power has remained more or less unaffected in Iron and Steel Industry due to liberalization process came into operation.

Suppliers' Power

Competition in an industry increases/decreases with the decrease/ increase in suppliers' power. Suppliers' power exists in its extreme form in industries with monopolies (large number of buyers and few sellers) which enables manufacturers to charge extra prices on goods.

In iron and steel industry, a significant reduction in suppliers' power has been mainly due to removal of licensing restriction and relaxation of equity participation norms which have led to availability of greater funds for the setting up of economic size plants.

Threat of Substitutes

Competition in an industry increases/decreases with greater or lesser availability of substitutes. Greater availability of substitutes enables customers to switch over among products offering similar benefits thereby increasing customers' bargaining power. The threat of substitutes in iron and steel industry has increased mainly on account of reduction in tariff barrier on metal and setting up of large scale capacities. This has increased competition for metal sector in general and Iron and Steel Industry in particular.

Entry Barrier

Competition in an industry increases/decreases with decrease/increase in entry barriers. Entry barriers impose restrictions on the number of players in the Industry. Pre-reform entry barrier was on account of licensing of capacities, high import duties on capital goods, restriction on FDI and equity participation and restriction on external borrowing. But, removal of capacity restrictions has led to large scale capacity addition as is witnessed in steel industry. Therefore, reduction in suppliers' power coupled with reduced entry barriers and increased threat from substitutes has induced increased competition for manufacturers in Iron and Steel Industry.

Table 6: Porter Model: Changes in the degree of Competition in Indian Iron and Steel Industry during post-1991

Sector	Buyers' Power	Suppliers' Power	Threat of Substitutes	Entry Barrier	Competition
Iron and Steel	⇔	↓	↑	↓	↑

Using Porter model, we have concluded that competition in Iron and Steel Industry has been increased during the post-reform period.

Despite competitiveness of a firm can be judged in view of concentration ratio a firm in an industry occupies during a particular period of time, it is not the reliable parameter in evaluating competitive scenario as because the position of the firms in the industry may have variations keeping concentration ratio same.

Ijiri and Simon (1977) elucidate that a "frequent and sizeable change in the ranks of the firms in an industry would indicate vigorous competition in the industry. On the other hand, if the ranks do not change frequently, it is an indication of little competition. To understand the intensity of competition, in view of Baldwin and R. John (1998), frequent changes in relative firm's position in the industry explicitly indicates the prevalence of intense competition.

Ijiri and Simon suggest a measure of competition which is based on the relative ranks of firms at two different point of time. The initial and terminal period for the analysis of competition are considered. This measure is termed as the standard duration of $q_i = r_i/r_i^*$, where r_i is the rank at the end of a period and r_i^* is the rank at the beginning of the period. The standard deviation of q is an indicator of the average amount of shifting in rank[7] during the period. Within the post-liberalized time frame of 1991-92 to 2004-05, effort done by Ijiri and Simon (1977) has been adopted for 9 firms in Indian iron and steel sector for the two consecutive years at the beginning, 1990-91 and 1991-92 as well as at the end, 2003-04 and 2004-05. Thereafter, standard deviations of relative ranks have been estimated using Ijiri -Simon Index method for the terminal points to have insight into the mode of competition. It is evident from

Table 7 below that out of 9 firms in Indian Iron and Steel Industry, average shifting has come down in 4 firms, which indicates that competition has declined substantially. In two firms (alloy steel and fabricated steel structural excluding transmission tower), average shifting remains same between these two time periods and in remaining 3 firms, average shifting has increased implying increase in competition. Decline in competition varies from 20 per cent to 83 per cent whereas increase in competition fluctuates from 32 per cent to 106 per cent. The highest decline in average shifting occurs in Iron Sponge and lowest decline in Steel Pipe and Tubes. At the same time, highest increase in average shifting occurs in Steel and lowest increases in Metal Containers. The above analysis of competition compels us to conclude that pattern of increase/decrease in competition varies among firms within the said industry. We have a rank correlation of 0.2472 between average shifting at the two end points, which suggests that position of various firms in Indian Iron, and steel industry with regard to competition seems to have no significant change. This is because of the fact that this particular industry is operated with assured margins, protected against the emergence of competition from within India through licensing or from across the boarders through high import tariff which keep Indian Iron and Steel Industry outside the purview of competition. Average rank shifting for the entire industry for the two terminal periods is declining (from 0.40 to 0.17).

Table 7: Ijiri-Simon Index of Competition

Industry's Sub-Sectors	*Standard Deviation of Relative Rank*		*% Change*
	1991-92/ 1990-91	*2004-05/ 2003-04*	
Iron Sponge	0.3572(8)	0.059(4)	-83.48
Pig Iron	2.03(9)	0.421(9)	-79.26
Steel	0.1843(3)	0.380(8)	106.18
Ferro Alloy	0.2161(6)	0.324(7)	49.93
Alloy Steel	0.1070(2)	0.107(5)	00
Fabricated Steel Structural excluding Transmission Tower	00(1)	00(2)	00
Metal Container	0.1844(4)	0.2430(6)	31.78
Steel Pipe and Tubes	0.2060(5)	00(2)	-20.60
Steel Wire and Ropes	0.2658(7)	00(2)	-26.58
Average	0.3945	0.1704	

Note: Figures in the parenthesis indicate respective rank order. r = 0.2472

Source: Own estimate.

6. Threats of Liberalization

The opening-up of Indian economy to global competitive forces is posing new challenges and opportunities to Indian manufacturers. It may lead to the emergences of global monopolies and in this process there are chances of many domestic Indian companies being swallowed up by foreign giants. Inviting foreign steel makers in India allowing free import of steel will certainly enhance a sense of competition among the Indian steel makers. Some of the big steel producers of U.S.A., Japan and European countries and also China have abundant research and development facilities which cannot be matched in our iron and steel plants. This unmatched disparity would surely generate uneven competition.

Secondly, there may be cases of unfair trade practices like dumping of steel products. Thirdly, unconditional foreign participation may lead to huge dividend repatriation from India. Fourthly, successful globalization requires macro-economic stability. In an unsuccessful macro economic situation, it may initiate huge loss of trade resulting from price disadvantages (Haleem, 1996).

Policy Measures to be Adopted

Liberalization being an ongoing process is continuously changing the national economic scenario. Indian Iron and Steel Industry is being forced to change its dimension for its survival. Therefore, competitive environment resulting from liberalization is bound to affect the future course of Iron and Steel Industry. The trend towards globalization of steel industry is characterized by large scale privatization, greater international participation, increased emphasis on market orientation in terms of product quality etc. The steel industry has always shown a tendency of competitive investment and modernization. Consequently, there is an urgent need for developing a strategic plan for the Indian Iron and Steel Industry.

(1) Adoption of a wide-ranging plan for modernization of all existing steel plants should be given priority in order to be competitive in global perspective.
(2) As a result of lowering down of import and export duties, development of a trigger mechanism against dumping of iron and steel and also allied products is of crucial need.
(3) Iron and steel being a mature industry offers many good

opportunities of expanding business through the chain of acquisition and merger as are taking place worldwide. This strategic tie-up will not only provide better assurance to investors but also strengthen assets and absolute liquidity position of consolidated entity to draw more funds.

(4) Liberalization can be successful only in the long-run when proper infrastructure is available. Therefore development of infrastructure facilities will flow the demand of steel product.

(5) Iron and steel is the world's most recycled material whose recycle ability makes it ecologically desirable alternative from both producers and customers viewpoint. Recycling of one tonne of steel scrap saves: iron ore 1.5 tonnes, coke 1 tonnes, lime stone 0.5 tonne, and reduces air pollution by 85 per cent, water pollution 76 per cent, and mining waste 97 per cent. So scrap collection and recycling industry should be developed in Indian scenario.

(6) Restructuring in a technology centric sense has often been referred to as 'elimination of older facilities', the modernization of remaining facilities and a balancing of net capacity with market demand. With privatization inevitable, it is important to restructure PSU of steel industry to derive maximum benefit in terms of increased value creation.

(7) Established and cash rich players went out modernizing their facilities even when there was life left in the older equipment in order to retain their position in the market taking advantage of superior quality and operational cost associated with the modern plant. But, for the most, technology upgradation proved a mammoth task despite the fact that they are facing death otherwise. Therefore, to compete globally, R&D for the development of technology should be promoted urgently.

(8) This industry all over world has cried for protection so that their home market earnings can be enhanced, when direct and tariff barriers are not possible, the industry seeks non-tariff protection almost everywhere especially in India where the industry is in deep financial crisis and it should be provided immediately.

(9) There is an urgent need of direct state subsidies by domestic government. to this industry to maintain high level of export at low prices defying the real strength and nature of global competition because direct state intervention and increasing

support of it to the industry literally provides assurance that the state will come to its rescue whenever needed.

7. Summary and Conclusion

The main findings of the present article are summarized below:

There was a slight decline in average capacity utilization rate in post-reform period as compared to pre-reform period. Annual average growth rate of capacity output and actual output show similar increasing trend but output grows at a much slower rate than capacity output. Our analysis regarding trend in capacity utilization suggests that the higher rate of capacity creation can be attributed to the huge amount of public investment during post-reform period made in this sector which provides supply side support to Indian Iron and Steel Industry. Therefore, the trend in capacity expansion reflects that capacity expanded more rapidly in post-reform period than in pre-reform period. Removal of industrial licensing restriction might have encouraged the entrepreneurs to invest more and expand their plant capacity. The liberalization process is found to have its significant adverse impact on capacity utilization since there is a fall in average growth rate of capacity utilization during the post-reform period. Rank shifting measure suggested by Ijiri-Simon which is tested for 9 firms in Indian Iron and Steel Industry for a period of 14 years after liberalization process started reveals that nearly half of the firms in the industry have shown a declining trend in competition. Rank correlation of change in rank-shifting does not show significant shift in their relative position during post-reform period indicating existence of rigidity in the expansion of competition in Indian Iron and Steel Industry which is also contrary to common expectation.

The present study suffers from certain limitations, which should be taken into account while interpreting the results. Due to non-availability of data on periodic price series of energy in India, some approximations have taken into account. There is also a key limitation of the study that it assumes capital to be homogeneous in nature while it has distinct identifiable components. Aggregating these components at historical prices, deflating by a single index number and assuming all components to follow a uniform rate of depreciation and longevity may induce some amount of bias into the level of capital input. The labour variable used in the study, total persons engaged, is a concept of stock whereas its flow counterpart is man-hours used in the production process. But, Annual Survey of Industries (ASI) does not provide data on man-hours. The input-output table, which is used for the construction of energy input deflator, is for both the registered and unregistered sector, even though the study covers the registered sector only.

In conclusion, it is suggested that aggregate growth strategies through stimulation of domestic demand, access to global market, investment in new emerging growth areas are required for propelling a higher growth rate. Consolidation is the urgent need to achieve higher scale of operation in order to compete efficiently in liberalized regime as well as to face global challenges.

NOTES

1. Till 1988 – 89, the classification of industries followed in ASI was based on the National Industrial classification 1970 (NIC 1970). The switch to the NIC-1987 from 1989-90 and also switch to NIC1998 requires some matching. Considering NIC1987 as base and further NIC 1998 as base, Iron &Steel industry has been treated as 330 coded industry and 2710 coded industry respectively. For price correction of variable, wholesale price indices taken from official publication of CMIE have been used to construct deflators.
2. Griliches and Ringstad (1971) have preferred GVA to gross output and reasons for imposing preference have been mentioned in their study.
3. To compute the price of energy inputs, some studies have aggregated quantities of different energy inputs using some conversion factors (say British Thermal units or coal replacement etc.) and then take the ratio of expenditure on energy to the aggregate quantity of energy. This method is criticized because it assumes different types of energy inputs to be perfect substitutes.
4. Prime lending rate is generally viewed as an opportunity cost of capital, but problem is that there is no unique lending rate available for use. So, we have used rate of interest on long term government bond and securities as rate of return on capital [as previously used by Jha, Murty and Paul (1991)].Alternatively, one can use the gross yield on preferential industrial shares, if available, as Murty (1986) has done.
5. As Jorgenson and Griliches note capital gains should be deducted from $(r_t + d_t)$ but several studies have not done so and adjustment for capital gains does not seem to make such difference to the result.
6. Tobin (1969) defines q as the ratio of the market value to the replacement cost of the firm's capital stock. Berndt and Fuss(1986) have shown that Tobin's q can be written as Z_k/P_k where Z_k is $\partial VC/\partial K$ and CU and Tobin's q are positively related .Since $\partial 2VC/\partial K\partial(K/Y)$ is b_{KK}, which is positive,

therefore $\partial q/\partial(K/Y)$ is negative. So, industry with high levels of *K/Y* will have, other things remaining same, low levels of CU.

7. Rank shifting has been judged in view of top 10 companies' sales performance within each and every firm of Indian Iron &Steel Industry.

REFERENCES

1. Ahluwalia, I.J. 1985, *Industrial Growth in India*, Oxford University Press, Delhi.
2. Abdul Azeez, Erumban (2005), Economic reform and industrial performance: an analysis of capacity utilization in Indian manufacturing, *Indian Journal of Economics and Business,* December, vol.4 (2), pp.305-323.
3. Baldwin, R. John (1998), *The Dynamics of Industrial Competition*, a *North American Perspective*, Cambridge University Press, UK.
4. Balakrishnan, P. and K. Pushpangadan (1994), Total factor productivity growth in manufacturing industry: A fresh look, *Economic and Political Weekly,* July 30.
5. Barik, Kaustava (2007), Capacity utilization in Indian paper industry, *Working paper, School of Social Science*, Indira Gandhi National Open University.
6. Berndt, E.R. and Fuss, M.A. (1981): Productivity measurement using capital asset valuation to adjust for variation in utilization (*Paper presented at the Econometric Society Summer Meetings*, San Diego, C.A.)
7. —— (1981): Capacity utilization: underlying economic theory and an alternative approach, *American Economic Review*, 71, (22), 48-52.
8. Chaturvedi, D.N. and Amaresh Bagchi (1984) Age Structure of Fixed capital in the Indian Economy, 1970-71 to 1980-81, *Journal of Income and Wealth,* Vol. 7, No. 1: 82-83.
9. Cassel, J.M. (1937), Excess capacity and monopolistic competition, *Quarterly Journal of Economics,* 51, 426-443.
10. Denny, M., M. Fuss and L. Waverman, 'Substitution possibilities for Energy; Evidence from U.S. and Canadian manufacturing Industries in E.R. Berndt and B.C. Field, *Modelling and Measuring National Resources Substitution* (Cambridge M.A., MIT Press, 1981).
11. Das, Debkusum (2004), Manufacturing productivity under varying trade regime, 1980-2000, *Economic and Political Weekly*, January, 31, pp. 423-33.
12. Johansen, L. (1968). Production Functions and the Concept of Capacity, Namur, Recherches Récentes sur la Fonction de Production (Collection "Economie Mathématique et Econometrie", n° 2) [reprinted in F.R. Førsund (ed.) (1987). *Collected Works of Leif Johansen, Volume 1,* Amsterdam, North Holland,359-382].

13. Fare. R., S. Grosskopf, and E. Kokkelenberg. (1989). "Measuring Plant Capacity, Utilization and Technical Change: A Non-parametric Approach,' *International Economic Review*, 30: 655-666.
14. Färe, R. (1994). "The Existence of Plant Capacity," *International Economic Review*, 25: 209-213.
15. Friedman, M. (1963), More on Archibald versus Chicago, *Review of Economic Studies,* 30, 65-67.
16. Jorgenson, Dale, W. and Zvi Griliches, 'The explanation of productivity change; *Review of Economic Studies* 34 (1967), 249-282.
17. Klein, L.R., 'Some theoretical issues in the measurement of capacity', *Econometrica,* 28, (April 1960), 272-286.
18. Krishna, K.L. (1972), 'Industrial capacity and production in C.R. Rao, *Database of Industrial Economy* Vol. 1, New Delhi.
19. Gajanan, Shailendra and D. Malhotra (2007), Measures of capacity utilization and its determinants: a study of Indian manufacturing, *Applied Economics*, Vol. 39, Issue 6, April, pp. 765-776.
20. Gasper, A. Garofalo and Devinder, M. Malhotra, Regional measure of capacity utilization in the 1980s. *The Review of Economics and Statistics* Vol. 34, 415-421.
21. Goldar, B.N., V.S. Ranganathan, Rashmi Banga (2004); Capacity utilization in Indian Industries, *Indian Economic Journal,* (91), 39(2), 82-89.
22. Gort, M. (1963): Analysis of Stability and change in market share, *Journal of Political Economy,*71, February, pp. 51-63.
23. Goldar, and V.S. Ranganathan, (1991); Capacity utilization in Indian Industries, *Indian Economic Journal,* 39(2), Oct-Dec, 82-92.
24. Goldar, Biswanath and V.S. Renganathan (2008), Import penetration and capacity utilization in Indian industries, Working paper series no. E/293/ 2008., *Institute of Economic Growth*, New Delhi.
25. Greliches, Z. and Y. Ringstad (1971); *Economics of scale and the form of the production function*, North Holland, Amsterdam.
26. Hashim, A. Danish (2003), Capacity Utilization in Indian Airlines, Working paper, *Institute of Economic Growth*, Delhi.
27. Ijiri, Y. and H.A. Simon (1977): *Skewed Distribution and the Size of Business*. North Holland, Amsterdam.
28. Joskow, J. (1960): Structural Indicia: Rank Shifting Analysis as a supplement to concentration ratios, *Review of Economics and Statistics*, Vol. XLII, pp. 113-16.
29. Kumar Sunil and Nitin Arora (2009), Analyzing Regional Variations in Capacity Utilization of Indian Sugar Industry using Non-parametric Frontier Technique, *Eurasian Journal of Business and Economics,* 2 (4), pp. 1-26.
30. Morrison, C.J., 1985, 'On the Economic Interpretation and measurement of optimal capacity; *Review of Economic Studies*, (1985) LII, 295-310.

31. Nelson, R.A. (1989), On the measurement of capacity utilization, *The Journal of Industrial Economics,* vol. XXXVII, March, 1989.
32. Paul, S. 1974, 'Growth and capacity utilization of Industrial capacity; *Economic and Political Weekly,* December 7, pp. 2025 -2032.
33. Segerson, Katherine and Dale Squires.(1990). On the Measurement of Economic Capacity Utilization for Multi-Product Industries, *Journal of Econometrics*, Vol. 44:347-361.
34. Sastry, D.U. 1984, *The Cotton Mill Industry in India,* Oxford University Press, Delhi.
35. Srinivasan, P.V., 'Determinants of Capacity utilization in Indian Industries', *Journal of Quantitative Economics,* Vol. 8, No. 1 (1992) 139-156.
36. Uchikawa, S., 'Investment boom and underutilization of capacity in the 1990s, *Economic and Political Weekly,* August 25, 2001, pp. 3247–3253.
37. V. Bhanu, Liberalization and Performance of Cement Industry, *Economic and Political Weekly,* August 26, 1995.

Appendix

A-1 Energy Inputs

Industry level time series data on cost of fuel of Indian Iron and Steel sector have been deflated by suitable deflator (base 1981-82 = 100) to get real energy inputs. An input-output table provides the purchase made by manufacturing industry from input-output sectors. These transactions are used as the basis to construct weight and then weighted average of price index of different sectors is taken. Taking into consideration 115 sector input-output table (1998-99) prepared by CSO, the energy deflator is formed as a weighted average of price indices for various input-output sectors which considers the expenses incurred by manufacturing industries on coal, petroleum products and electricity as given in I-O table for 1998-99. The WIP indices (based 1981-82) of Coal, Petroleum and Electricity have been used for these three categories of energy inputs. The columns in the absorption matrix for 66 sectors belonging to manufacturing (33-98) have been added together and the sum so obtained is the price of energy made by the manufacturing industries from various sectors. The column for the relevant sector in the absorption matrix provides the weights used.

A2 Capital Stock

The procedure for the arriving at capital stock series is depicted as follows:

First, an implicit deflator for capital stock is formed on NFCS at current and constant prices given in NAS. The base is shifted to 1981-82 to be consistent with the price of inputs and outputs.

Second, an estimate of Net Fixed Capital Stock (NFCS) for the registered manufacturing sector for 1970-71 (benchmark) is taken from National Accounts Statistics. It is multiplied by a gross-net factor to get an estimate of Gross Fixed Capital Stock (GFCS) for the year 1970-71. The rate of gross to net fixed asset available from RBI bulletin was 1.86 in 1970-71 for medium and large public Ltd. companies. Therefore, the NFCS for the registered manufacturing for the benchmark year (1970-71) as reported in NAS is multiplied by 1.86 to get an estimate of GFCS which is deflated by implicit deflator at 1981-82 prices to get it in real figure. In order to obtain benchmark estimate of gross real fixed capital stock made for registered manufacturing, it is distributed among various two digit industries (in our study, Iron and Steel Industry in proportion of its fixed capital stock reported in ASI, 1970-71)

Third, from ASI data, gross investment in fixed capital of iron and Steel Industry in India is computed for each year by subtracting the book value of fixed asset in previous year from that in the current year and adding to that figure the reported depreciation of the fixed asset in current year and subsequently it is deflated by the implicit deflator to get real gross investment. (Symbolically, $I_t = (B_t - B_{t-1} + D_t)/P_t$) Fixed capital represents the depreciated value of fixed assets owned by the factory as on the closing day of the accounting year. Fixed capital covers all types of assets, new or used or own constructed, deployed for production, transportation, living or recreational facilities, hospitals, schools etc. for factory personnel. It also includes the fixed assets of the head office allocable to the factory and also the full value of assets taken on hire purchase basis (whether fully paid or not) excluding interest elements. It excludes intangible assets and assets solely used for post-manufacturing activities.

Fourth, the post-benchmark real gross fixed capital stock is arrived at by the following procedure. Real gross fixed capital stock (t) = real gross fixed capital stock (t – 1) + real gross investment (t). Goldar (1986) talks of various possibilities with regard to the rate of discarding of assets. This may be zero, a constant or a fraction of previous year's fixed capital stock. In our study, the annual rate of discarding of capital stock (D_{st}) is assumed to be zero due to difficulty in obtaining data regarding D_{st}.

6

Environmental Performance and its Determinants: A Study on Pulp and Paper Industry in India

Sebak Kumar Jana and *Debasish Barik*

The pulp and paper industry is based on chemical process with major impact on environment. Pulp and paper are manufactured from raw materials containing cellulose fibres, generally wood, recycled paper, and agricultural residues. In developing countries, about 60 per cent of cellulose fibres originate from non-wood raw materials. The first paper mill in India was set up at Sreerampur, West Bengal, in the year 1812. In India paper mills are of three types based on raw material use— forest based mills, agro-residue based mills and recycled fibre, i.e. waste paper based mills. Forest-based raw materials consist of bamboo and mixed tropical hardwood extracted from natural forests. Agro-residues consist of cereal straw, *sarkanda*, *sabai* grass and sugarcane bagasse. Wood-based production still dominates the paper industry in India. Because of the severe shortage of forest raw material and agro-waste/residues such as rice straw and wheat straw and bagasse are relatively short cycled regenerative and abundant, the utilization of agricultural residues has increased substantially since 1970s. Wastepaper is chief source of raw materials for small paper mills to produce primarily low quality paper such as kraftpaper and paperboard. Despite the relatively high collection costs, wastepaper is a cheap source of fibre. The contribution of forest-based, agro-based and others (wastepaper secondary fibre, bast fibres and market pulp) are respectively 42.9, 28.1 and 29 per cent. Pulp mills and paper mills may exist separately or as integrated operations. Effluents from pulp and paper mills pollute water, air and land. From the input side it consumes water, raw materials like forest resources, agro-residues, chemicals and various energy resources. In the output side along with paper it generates pollutants like black liquor, colour etc. Nature of different pollutants depends on the production process employed. Pollution generated at various stages of production of pulp and paper due to input use and potential environmental impact are shown in Table 1.

Table 1: Simplified Process Flow Chart Showing the Major Process Steps in Chemical Pulping and Bleaching and Environmental Impact

Main Input	*Process Step*	*Potential Environmental Impact*
Fibre raw material	Handling fibre raw material	Solid waste
Chemicals, Energy	Pulping (Recovery)	Gaseous material, Water vapour
Water	Washing	Dissolved material, Residual chemicals
Energy	Screening	Solid Waste
Chemicals, Energy	Bleaching	Dissolved material, residual chemicals
Energy	Dyeing	
Energy, Water, Chemicals	Paper Machine	Solid waste, Dissolved material, residual chemicals

Source: UNEP (2000).

The pulp and paper industry is under the list of seventeen most polluting sectors as identified by the Central Pollution Control Board of India (CPCB, 2001). Annual pollution load of different industries is presented in Table 2. The annual pollution load of paper industry is 4.59 per cent of the Total pollution load in India.

There is an extensive literature on pollution abatement behaviour of firms. Some of these are mentioned below. Despite widely acknowledged weaknesses of the regulatory framework in developing countries, it has been seen plants exhibit great variety in environmental performance, i.e. behaviour of firms differ.

Table 2: Annual Pollution Load of Different Industries in India

	BOD (Tonnes)	*Percentage*
Iron and Steel	16,39,368	87.24
Pulp and Paper	86,245	4.59
Aluminium	47,469	2.53
Fertilisers	31,480	1.68
Sugar	16,747	0.89
Copper	16,035	0.85
Distillery	7,740	0.41
Zinc	7,737	0.41
Pesticides	7,366	0.39
Drugs	5,889	0.31
Cement	5,168	0.28
Oil Refinery	4,340	0.23
Petrochemicals	1,818	0.10
Leather	894	0.05
Caustic Soda	836	0.04
Total	18,79,132	100.0

Source : Madia (2003).

The paper by Hettige *et al.* (1996) reviews evidence drawn from three empirical studies of plant-level abatement practices conducted 1992-94. The analysis tests the importance of plant characteristics, economic considerations and external pressure in determining environmental performance. Pargal *et al.* (1997) uses survey data from industrial plants to examine regulatory inspections and water pollution emissions in India, and to check whether the monitoring and enforcement efforts of provincial pollution control authorities are affected by local community characteristics. This paper shows that high levels of pollution elicit a formal regulatory response in the form of inspections on emissions, underlining the institutional failures. EIU (1993) offers a premier suitable for companies in transition and on the leading edge of corporate greening, with hundreds of practical examples of how executives across all functions are meeting the challenges of sustainable development. Chen *et al.* (1998) examines the impact of economic and demographic variables on generation and treatment of four classes of polluting residuals from industrial production in China. Afash *et al.* (1996) have argued for a broader model which includes the community and the market as major players in the determination of factories' environmental performance. Roles of communities, markets and governments in controlling industrial pollution have been elaborately discussed in World Bank (1999). Green Rating Project of CSE (1999, 2004) has rated the pulp and paper sector in India. The main purpose of the project was to rank different paper companies according to their environmental performance. The 2004 CSE report claims that public disclosure of rating in 1999 has a definite influence on the environmental performance of the other mills. This supports the influence of informal regulations on pollution abatement actions of paper plants. Kathuria (2004) examines the importance of informal regulation in controlling industrial pollution in a developing country like India. Informal regulations can take various forms like demands for compensation by community groups, social ostracism of the polluting firm's employees, the threat of physical violence, efforts to monitor and publicise the firm's emissions/discharges, reporting violation of standards to the regulatory agencies, putting pressure on regulator (through politicians and administrators) to tighten monitoring and enforcement, public disclosure, ratings etc. The paper investigates whether the press has any role to play in pollution control in the second most industrialised state of India, i.e. Gujarat. However study by Jana and Roy (2006) shows that in West Bengal formal regulation play a role in inducing pollution control behaviour in pulp and paper mills. With the evidences drawn from American and Canadian studies, Lanoie *et al.* (1998) concludes that capital markets react to the release of information of polluter's environmental performance, and that large polluters are affected more significantly from such release than smaller polluters.

Though there is extensive literature on this issue of industrial pollution, there is a limited number of empirical studies using plant level data in the Indian context for environmental performance analysis. We have selected Pulp and Paper Industry in India for our study.

Objectives of the Paper

The present study is based on the data collected from primary survey. Our broad objective is to look into the environmental performance of paper mills under our study. The main objectives of the paper are as follows:

(1) To look into the different economic and environmental aspects of paper mills, like production process, raw material consumption pattern, environmental performance indicators etc.

(2) To investigate the determinants of environmental performance and to see whether there is any relationship between economic efficiency and environmental performance measured in terms of pollution intensity of firms under consideration.

Methodology and Data Source

As we have stated one of our objectives is to see whether there is any relationship between environmental efficiency and economic efficiency. We have used data envelopment analysis for deriving economic efficiency of the paper mills and to investigate the determinants of environmental efficiency we have used regression analysis. The primary data had been collected from 16 paper mills from two states of India, namely West Bengal and Uttar Pradesh. The data has been collected on the basis of structured questionnaire designed for the purpose. The survey primary was conducted during 2006-07.

Description of the Characteristics of the Mills

We have collected information about different characteristics of the plants including environmental and economic characteristics. Out of the 16 plants surveyed most of the plants produce Kraft Paper or board with one mill producing newsprint and one mill producing cream wove. Mill-wise Type of produce, raw materials used and process of production is reported in Table 3. Most of the mills are wastepaper based mills and use hydrapulping process.

Some descriptive statistics of the plants are presented in Table 4. The average amount of the sample 16 plants for different characteristics are as follows: Paper production — 12,310 MT, Sales — Rs. 247 million, Employment in the production sector (PE)— 148, Annual wage of production employees — Rs. 6.9 million, Annual wage per production employee — 51,606, percentage of product exported (PEXP) — 5 per cent and age of the plant — 18. Most of the plant produce to meet the domestic demand. As the age of the plant shows the oldest plant of our sample is of 52 years.

Table 3: Plant-wise type of Paper Produced, Raw Materials Used and Production Process

Mill	*Type of Paper*	*Type of Raw Materials*	*Process*
Mill 1	News print, cream wove	Waste Paper (domestic and imported)	Soda
Mill 2	Duplex board	Waste Paper (domestic)	Kraft pulping
Mill 3	Duplex board, bray board	Waste Paper	Hydrapulping
Mill 4	Duplex board	Waste Paper (domestic and imported)	Waste Paper process
Mill 5	Absorbent paper, Kraft paper	Bagasse, Waste Paper (domestic and imported), Imported pulp	Soda and hydrapulping
Mill 6	Kraft paper	Straw, bagasse, waste paper (domestic)	Soda
Mill 7	Media kraft paper	Waste paper (domestic)	Hydrapulping
Mill 8	Kraft paper	Bagasse, waste paper (domestic)	Soda
Mill 9	Kraft paper	Waste paper (domestic and imported)	Lime process
Mill 10	Kraft paper	Straw, bagasse, waste paper (domestic)	Hydrapulping
Mill 11	Kraft paper	Waste paper (domestic and imported)	Waste Paper process
Mill 12	Duplex board, kraft paper	Straw, bagasse, waste paper (domestic)	Chemical soda process/hydrapulping
Mill 13	Kraft paper	Waste paper (domestic)	Hydrapulping
Mill 14	Duplex board	Bagasse, waste paper (domestic)	Soda
Mill 15	Kraft paper	Straw, bagasse, waste paper (domestic)	Hydrapulping
Mill 16	Cream wove	Straw, waste paper (domestic and imported)	Sulphite

Source: Primary Survey.

Table 4: Descriptive Statistics of the Primary Survey

	Average	*Standard Deviation*	*Maximum*	*Minimum*
PP (MT)	12,320	6746	23760	3200
S (million)	247	168	602	35
PE	148	97	350	30
W (million)	6.9	6.5	24.66	1.2
Wage rate	51606	22784	81111	5000
PEXP	5	11	30	0
AGE	18	12	52	5

Source: Based Primary Survey Data.

Major raw materials used per tonne of paper production is reported in Table 5. Mills are using different raw materials like straw, bagasse, waste-paper (both domestic and imported). Water consumption per tonne of paper production (measured in cubic metre per tonne of paper) is reported in the last column of the table. The mills using virgin raw materials for producing paper use greater amount of water compared to mills using waste-paper.

Table 5: Raw Materials used (in tonnes) per Tonne of Paper Production

	Straw	*Bagasse*	*Waste-Paper (Domestic)*	*Waste-paper (Imported)*	*Water (M^3/tonne of paper)*
Mill 1	0	0	0.09	0.00	22.23
Mill 2	0	0	1.35	0.00	15
Mill 3	0	0	0.00	0.00	18
Mill 4	0	0	0.12	1.14	9
Mill 5	0.25	0.25	1.27	0.29	6
Mill 6	0.25	0.25	0.90	0.00	15
Mill 7	0	0	0.81	0.00	10
Mill 8	0	0.70	0.70	0.00	13
Mill 9	0	0	1.45	0.01	28
Mill 10	0	0	0.00	0.00	18
Mill 11	0	0	1.08	0.31	18
Mill 12	0.01	0.06	0.00	0.00	15
Mill 13	0	0.00	1.05	0.00	14
Mill 14	0	0.33	1.03	0.00	15
Mill 15	0.34	0.19	1.26	0.00	14
Mill 16	1.8	0	0.25	0.25	120

Source: Calculated from Primary Survey Data.

The frequency distribution of firms according to employment size is presented in Table 6. The highest number of plants is in the range of employment of 51 to 100. The highest percentage of firms is in the range of (51-100).

Table 6: Employment Size Distribution of Plants

Employment Size	*No. of Firms*	*Percentage*
0-50	2	13
51-100	7	44
101-150	2	13
151-200	1	6
201-250	2	13
251-300	1	6
301-350	1	6
Total	16	100

Source: Based on Primary Survey Data.

Age of the plant is important from the pollution point of view. Older plants are supposed to be more polluting. The ageing pattern of the units is presented in Table 7. The age of the plants vary between 2 years and 51 years. As the age distribution shows, some of the plants are very young, though most of the plants are between 11 to 20 years of age.

Table 7: Age Distribution of the Plants

Age (Year)	*No. of Firms*	*Percentage*
(0-5)	1	6
(6-10)	1	6
(11-20)	10	63
(21-30)	2	13
(31-40)	0	0
(41-50)	1	6
(51-60)	1	6
Total	16	100

Source: Based on Primary Survey Data.

The type of boiler, energy consumption, solid waste generation for the sample paper mills is reported in Table 8. Most of the paper mills use coal fired boiler. Energy consumption varies widely across firms with highest of 13.1 Kcal/tonne for Mill 13. The generation of solid wastes per day is reported in the last column. In general the entire range of solid wastes in the industry can be divided into two broad categories, viz., cellulosic and inorganic. The highest solid waste generation measured in tonnes per day is 27.5 tonnes per day for mill 4.

Table 8: Boiler Type, Energy Use and Solid Waste Generation in the Paper Mills

	Type of boiler	*Energy Kcal/Tonne*	*Solid waste (Tonnes/day)*
Mill 1	Coal fired (Fluidised bed)	0.8	7.0
Mill 2	Husk fired	1.0	0.5
Mill 3	Coal fired	1.2	2.8
Mill 4	Coal fired, Multi fuel boiler	2.0	27.5
Mill 5	Coal fired, Multi fuel boiler	0.8	8.0
Mill 6	Coal and Baggasse fired	3.9	1.0
Mill 7	Coal fired boiler	1.2	2.1
Mill 8	Baggasse, wood	3.1	5.0
Mill 9	Multi Fuel type	1.3	3.2
Mill 10	Coal fired, Multi fuel boiler	3.6	11.0
Mill 11	Coal fired, Multi fuel boiler	5.3	14.5
Mill 12	Coal and Husk fired	5.9	17.5
Mill 13	Baggasse	13.1	6.5
Mill 14	Multi Fuel boiler	8.3	3.0
Mill 15	Multi fuel boiler	5.0	11.0
Mill 16	Coal fired (FBC)	4.0	8.3

Source: Based on Primary Survey Data.

The main sources of particulate emission are recovery furnace, lime kiln and power house boilers (CPCB, 1991). The mills under our study have taken different kinds of measures for controlling air pollution. The year of installation of different kinds of pollution control measures like Electro Static Precipitator (ESP), and bag filter have been given in Table 9. The monitoring of air quality measured by the number of visits by pollution control authority as reported by the plants is reported in the last column of Table 9.

Table 9: Year of Installation of Air Pollution Equipments

	Year of Installation	*Year of Installation*	*Monair*
Mill 1	—	1997	3
Mill 2	1992	—	4
Mill 3	—	2004	4
Mill 4	1998	—	24
Mill 5	1994	1994	12
Mill 6	—	—	8
Mill 7	1994	—	4
Mill 8	1994	1994	12
Mill 9	1995	1997	6
Mill 10	1993	1993	22
Mill 11	—	1996	24
Mill 12	2006	—	6
Mill 13	—	—	8
Mill 14	1990	—	22
Mill 15	1992	—	30
Mill 16	—	1997	2

Source: Based on Primary Survey Data.

The paper mills in India can be divided into three categories: large, medium and small. Mills with installed capacity of greater than 20,000 tonnes per annum (TPA) are defined as large mills. Mills with capacity between 10,000 TPA and 20,000 TPA are called medium paper mills. Small paper mills are those having capacity of less than 10,000 TPA. The average values for different parameters for large/medium and small paper mills have been calculated and have been presented in Table 10. The average production of the large/medium paper mills is 17,014 tonnes, and the average amount of production for small paper mills is calculated as 5,331 tonnes. Though COD intensity and BOD intensity is low in large/medium paper mills, water intensity is high for large paper mills. Energy intensity and number of Production Employees (PE) is almost same for both the groups. The average annual flow volume measured in Kilo litre per year (kly) is higher for smaller paper mills.

Water Pollution

Our environmental performance analysis will be mainly based on water pollution. We have collected information about different

Table 10: Average Values of Different Parameters for Large and Small Paper Mills

	Large/Medium	*Small*
Paper P (MT)	17014.5	5331.5
Sales (Rs. million)	317.1801	69.5891
COD (kg/Tonne)	1.410513	4.033011
BOD (kg/Tonne)	0.171885	1.21777
K (Rs. crore)	11.26137	2.865167
Age	21	16.66667
Export (%)	8	0
Energy (Kcal/kg)	3.876501	3.617676
Water (M^3/tonne of paper)	25.023	16.66667
Flow (kly)	1,06,162	1,19, 786
PE	138.9	137.1667

Source: Based on Primary Survey Data.

parameters of water pollution. All the plants have installed Effluent Treatment Plant (ETP) for the treatment of waste-water. We have collected data for water pollution parameters like BOD, COD, *p*H for both before treatment and after treatment. The descriptive statistics of the water pollution parametrers are presented in Table 11. The average value of different parameters before treatment of waste-water for our sample plants are as follows: BOD— 522.8 mg/l, COD – 997.2 mg/l, *p*H – 7.5, Suspended Solids (SS) – 1044.8 mg/l. As a result of installing ETP pollution has got reduced for all the mills. After treatment the average value of the parameters are as follows: BOD— 31.2 mg/l, COD – 170.4 mg/l, *p*H – 6.7, Suspended Solids (SS) – 78.6 mg/l. We have also collected data for flow size of waste-water going to ETP of all the mills. We have then calculated pollution load per tonne of paper production. The average value of pollution load measured in terms of BOD and COD per tonne of paper production are as follows: BOD – 0.364 kg/tonne and COD – 2.46 kg/tonne.

Plant-wise capital cost for ETP installation and operating cost for ETP is given in Table 12. The equipment cost for ETP ranges between 10 lakhs and 88 lakhs and the annual operating cost as has been calculated varies from Rs. 1.5 lakhs to Rs.18.3 lakhs. We have not received any data for ETP cost for mill 3.

Table 11: Descriptive Statistics of Water Pollution Parameters

		Average	*Standard Deviation*	*Maxi-mum*
Before Treatment	BOD (mg/l)	552.8	371.2	1400.0
	COD (mg/l)	997.2	407.1	1705.0
	*p*H	7.5	1.0	8.8
	SS (mg/l)	1044.8	876.8	3200.0
After Treatment	BOD (mg/l)	31.2	36.9	168.5
	COD (mg/l)	170.4	62.7	285.0
	*p*H	6.7	0.8	8.2
	SS (mg/l)	78.6	12.9	95.0
	BOD (Kg/T)	0.363953	0.5167	1.584
	COD (Kg/T)	2.461727	3.913037	12.078

Source: Based on Primary Survey Data.

Table 12: Capital Cost and Operating Cost of Effluent Treatment Plant (ETP)

	Capital Cost for ETP (Rs. Lakh)	*Operating Cost Rs. In Lakh per year*
Mill 1	61	8.8
Mill 2	13	1.5
Mill 3	—	—
Mill 4	45	9.6
Mill 5	60	18.3
Mill 6	10	3.7
Mill 7	12	3.5
Mill 8	14	0.8
Mill 9	24	7.2
Mill 10	45	11.0
Mill 11	45	7.2
Mill 12	50	7.3
Mill 13	40	7.3
Mill 14	35	7.3
Mill 15	50	14.6
Mill 16	88	17.5

Source: Primary Survey.

Efficiency of the Plants

We have used Data Envelopment Analysis (DEA) for judging the efficiency of the paper mills. The methodology was developed by Charnes, Cooper and Rhodes based on M.J. Farrel's contribution to productive efficiency. It is linear programming based technique for measuring the performance efficiency of a Decision Making Unit (DMU).

DEA models differ in the emphasis of their orientation (input oriented or output oriented) and on the assumption of returns to scale (CRS or VRS). Input-oriented DEA models tries to maximize the proportional decrease in input variables while remaining within the envelopment space (production possibility set), but output-oriented DEA models maximize the proportional increase in the output variables while remaining within the envelopment space. In other words input oriented technical efficiency is based on the question that how much input quantities be proportionally reduced without changing the output quantities produced. On the other hand, output oriented DEA is based on the question that how much output quantity be expanded without altering the input quantities used. Thus the possible improvement of an inefficient DMU could be achieved by either focusing on a proportional input reduction or proportional output augmentation or both simultaneously. Under VRS the envelopment surface presents convexity as a consequence of the constraint ($1\lambda = 1$) in the model. It ensures that the inefficient DMUs are measured in comparison with those efficient DMUs on the efficient frontier operating at the same scale size as themselves, the efficiency measured is 'pure technical efficiency' without considering the impact of the operating scale size of each DMU. The input-oriented VRS DEA model adopted in this study for input saving efficiency is an input-oriented VRS model as follows (Gang and Flemingham, 2002):

$$\text{Min } (\theta, \lambda, S+, S-)$$

$$TEc = \theta - \varepsilon\, (1s+ + 1s-)$$

$$\text{s.t. } Y\lambda - s+ = Yo$$

$$\theta x_0 - x\lambda - s^- = 0$$

$$1\lambda = 1$$

$$\lambda, s+, s^{-} \geq 0$$

Where TEc is the cost technical efficiency score and the variable θ is the (proportional) reduction applied to all inputs of DMU0 (the DMU being evaluated) to improve efficiency, λ is the value of constructing a composite unit with inputs Y λ and outputs X λ outperforming DMU_0, ε allows the minimization over θ to preempt the optimization involving the slack variables s+ and s^-, the variables s+ and s^- represent the excess inputs and output slacks and are the distance between an inefficient $DMU(X_0, Y_0)$ and its projected point on the envelopment surface of efficiency frontier.

Following the DEA methodology for input oriented VRS model we have derived the efficiency score of each paper mill under our study (Coelli, 1996). We have used a single output — gross sales including taxes and duties. The two inputs we have taken here for our analysis are gross block capital of the plant (K) and total wages paid to production employees (W). Gross block capital is defined as the sum total of all assets of the company valued at their cost of acquisition. The efficiency scores of the plants as derived from the analysis are reported in the last column of Table 13. As the results show there is huge variation of the efficiency scores of the plants. The average efficiency score is calculated as 0.769.

Regression Analysis

We have estimated the following regression equation on pollution intensity (measured in terms of kilograms of BOD per tonne of paper production). The independent variables in this equation are annual paper production of the plant measured in tonnes (PROD), Efficiency of the plant (EFF), wage rate of the production employee (WAGE) and monitoring of the waste-water by the pollution control authority (MONWW) measured in number of visits by pollution control authority.

$$\ln (BOD/PROD) = a_0 + a_1 \ln PROD + a_2 EFF + a_3 \ln WAGE + a_4 MONWW$$

We have collected data of PROD, W and MONW from the primary survey of plants. For the efficiency of the plants we have used the efficiency scores derived from DEA in the previous section.

Table 13: Plant-wise Output-Input Data and Efficiency Score

	Sales (Rs.millions)	*K (crores)*	*W (millions)*	*Eff Score (EFF)*
Mill 1	331.5	25.17	24.66	0.264
Mill 2	35	3.91	4.7	0.355
Mill 3	129.6	1.387	1.5	1
Mill 4	518.4165	15.33	6.104579	0.934
Mill 5	249.3757	4.47	5	0.937
Mill 6	36.8	1.527	2.5	0.908
Mill 7	46	2.5	1.225	1
Mill 8	180	5.96916	4.5	0.471
Mill 9	101.6346	6.34	1.2	1
Mill 10	395.2877	13.10853	6.273512	0.697
Mill 11	253.4608	4.896	6.72891	0.868
Mill 12	602.0599	15	6.6	1
Mill 13	68.5	1.527	6.8	0.908
Mill 14	174	1.8	4.5	1
Mill 15	186	2.87	6.9	0.756
Mill 16	281.7	24	21.9	0.217

Source: Based on Primary Survey Data.

Table 14: Regression Result of BOD Intensity

	Coefficients	*Standard Error*	*t Stat*	*P-value*
Intercept	1.94	5.32	0.37	0.72
lnPROD	-2.12	0.45	-4.75	0.00
EFF	-2.21	0.91	-2.42	0.03
lnWAGE	1.72	0.41	4.18	0.00
MONWW	-1.79	1.02	-1.75	0.11

Source: Estimation based on Primary Survey Data.

As the results in Table 14 show BOD intensity, i.e. pollution intensity has significant negative relation with production level, efficiency score, monitoring of waste-water by the pollution control authority. It has a positive significant relationship the wage rate.

Conclusion

We have tried to find the determinants of environmental performance of pulp and paper industry at firm level. The results suggest that size of the plant, the wage rate, monitoring by pollution control authority and the economic efficiency of the plant are the main determining factors of the environmental performance of the plants. We have measured here environmental performance in terms of BOD intensity. It should be pointed out that improved efficiency depends upon good operating practices which lead to better environmental performance of the plants. Improved efficiency enhances the possibility of better environmental performance. Formal regulation measured by monitoring has a role to play in controlling pollution intensity by the firms. The higher wage rate in our case is acting as disincentive for taking pollution control measures.

Acknowledgement: We owe greatly to Professor Joyashree Roy of the Department of Economics, Jadavpur University for her generous help at different levels of this work.

REFERENCES

1. Afash Shakeb *et al.* (1996), "Controlling Industrial Pollution: A New Paradigm", Policy Research Working Paper # 1672, *World Bank.*
2. Coelli Tim (1996), A Data Envelopment Analysis Computer Programme, *http://www.une.edu.au/econometrics/cepa.htm.*
3. CPCB (2000), Assessment of Industrial Pollution, http.//www.cpop.nic.In/pamsweb/assessindpolln.htm.
4. CSE (1999), "The Green Rating Project", *Down to Earth*, July 31.
5. CSE (1999), "The Green Rating Project", *Down to Earth*, July 31, pp. 20-51.
6. CSE (2004), "Who is India's Worst/Best Paper Maker?", *Down to Earth*, Oct. 15, 2004, pp. 27-42.
7. Gang, L. and B. Flemingham (2002), "The Technical Efficiency of Australian Irrigation Schemes", School of Economics, University of Tasmania, available in the website.
8. Ganguli, S. and J. Roy (1999), Water Pollution Abatement Cost and Tax in the Paper Industry, in G. Gupta and J. Roy (ed.), *Environmental Economics in India*, Allied Publishers Limited in Collaboration with Centre for Regional Economic Studies, Jadavpur University.
9. Hettige Hemamala *et al.* (1996), "Determinants of Pollution Abatement in Developing Countries: Evidence from South and Southeast Asia", *World Development*, Vol. 24, No. 12, pp. 1891-1904.
10. Jana, Sebak and Joyashree Roy (2004), "Polluting Industries in West Bengal: A Preliminary Analysis", *Vidyasagar University Journal of Economics*, 2004.
11. Jana, Sebak and Joyashree Roy (2006), "What Determines Pollution

Abatement Effort: Formal or Informal Regulation?" In A. Roy Chowdhury and J. Roy (ed.), *Development Challenges: Some Analytical Issues*, Allied Publishers.

12. Kathuria V. (2004), "Controlling Pollution in Small Industry", *Economic and Political Weekly*, June 26-July2, 2004, Vol. XXXIX, No. 26, pp. 2674-76.
13. Lanoic, P. (1998), "Can Capital Markets Create Incentives for Pollution Control?", *Ecological Economics*, Vol. 26, pp. 31-41.
14. Maria (2003) A., 'The Costs of Air Pollution in India', Paper Presented at the conference on Market Development of Water and Waste Technologies through Environmental Economics,' Delhi. http://www.cerna.ensmp.fr/Documents/cerna_globalisation/maria-delhi.pdf.
15. Pargal Sheoli, Muthukumara Mani and Mainul Huq (1997), "Inspections and Emissions in India: Puzzling Survey Evidence on Industrial Water Pollution", Policy Research Working Paper # 1810, *World Bank.*
16. Rock, M.T., Joyashree Roy, Sebak Jana and M. Kanjilal (2007): "Explaining Differences in Environmental Intensities in the Pulp and Paper Industry in India", Paper prepared for International START Secretariat, Available at the website, START NEDO full report, start.org/download/ITfinal.pdf.
17. Roy Joyashrree *et al.* (2008), *Natural Resource Accounting for West Bengal for the Sectors: Air and Water*, Submitted to Ministry of Statistics and Programme Implementation, Government of India, Global Change Programme, Jadavpur University, *http://mospi.gov.in/mospi_project_issp_ssd.htm.*
18. UNEP (2000), "United Nations Environment Programme: Industry and Environment", *Cleaner Production at Pulp and Paper Mills*, A Guidance Manual.
19. Wheeler David (1992), "The Economics of Industrial Pollution Control: An Alternative Perspective", Industry and Energy Department Working Paper, *World Bank*, Industry Series Paper No, 60.
20. World Bank (1999), "Greening Industry: New Roles for Communities, Markets and the Governments", New York, *World Bank*, Oxford University Press.
21. World Bank Group (1998): *Pollution Prevention and Abatement Handbook*, http://www.ifc.org/ifcext/enviro.nsf/AttachmentsByTitle/gui_pulp_WB/$FILE/pulp_PPAH.pdf.
22. Yap, N.T. and S.K. Awasthi (eds.)(1995), *Waste Management for Sustainable Development in India*, Tata McGraw-Hill Publishing Company Limited, New Delhi.

7

Swarnajayanti Gram Swarozgar Yojana (SGSY): Who Participates?

Arghya Kusum Mukharjee and *Amit Kundu*

Introduction

In spite of continued efforts over several decades, rural poverty in India is still significant. In each Five Year Plans, Government has introduced several anti-poverty programmes to reduce poverty. In percentage terms, poverty levels have reduced but the absolute number of rural poor has more or less remained static. The effect of such a large number of poor on the country's development is not difficult to see. Quite obviously, we need to redress the situation as quickly as possible. In this regard the Self-Employment Generation Programmes gain momentum because they can provide income to the rural poor on a sustainable basis, if planned properly and implemented rightly.

One of the most popular states promoted anti-poverty programme schemes is SGSY which is operative from 1st April, 1999 in rural areas of our country. SGSY scheme is an amalgamated version of six self-employed schemes, viz. IRDP, DWRCA, MWS, SITRA, GKY and TRYSEM. The scheme tries to establish a large number of Micro Enterprises or businesses in the rural area. The BPL households identified through BPL census and approved by Gramsabha forms the basis of identification. For BPL families the programme aims to ensure appreciable and sustained income over a period of time. This objective is being achieved by organizing the rural poor in Self-Help

Groups (SHGs) that are the grassroots level organizations. They are formed through the process of social mobilization provided with training and capacity building inputs and provision of income generating assets.

In some cases 20 per cent of the APL families and in exceptional cases 30 per cent of the group members may belong to APL families, but the APL members of the groups are not permitted to hold the position of office bearer and will not be entitled to get subside. 50 per cent of the group formed in each block should be exclusively for women who will account for at least 40 per cent of the Swarozgaris. This scheme is based on joint liability principle through forming Self-Help Groups. The group is formed sometimes through self-selection mechanism and sometimes through the initiative of local Panchayat, NGO or District Rural Development Authority (DRDA) of the State Government (Kundu, 2008). Initially each member has to contribute some amount to their respective group regularly. At least after six months of the formation of the group each SHG has to appear in a gradation test. The performance of a group depends on the average number of meetings arranged by the group in a particular month, regularity of the monthly contribution by all the members, regularity of the repayment of loans by the borrowing members etc. This gradation test is conducted in order to minimize the adverse selection problem, which may arise when the borrowers have characteristics that are unobservable to the lenders and that may affect the probability of the ability of loan repayment. Consequently the group has to go through II-gradation test, and ultimately they became eligible to get subsidy. As groups pass different gradation tests, they become eligible to get higher amount of credit (progressive lending).

Section II: Overview of Literature

The SGSY scheme has been designed on three features: joint liability, progressive lending and back ended subsidy. The existing economic research on group lending can be divided into two broad areas: (i) the theoretical analysis of the distinctive features of 'credit contracts' (like joint liability and dynamic incentives) with an emphasis on their implications for solving the adverse selection and moral hazard problems (See, for example, Stiglitz,1990, Besley and Coate,1995, Jain and Mansuri, 2003, Aghinon and Morduch,2005, Laffont and Rey, 2003), and (ii) the empirical analysis that focuses on the evolution of the effects of such programmes on the welfare of the borrowers, especially the women (See, for example, Pitt and Khandker,1998, Morduch, 1998).

Though the programme is in vogue for last nine years, there are meagre studies to provide comprehensive picture as well as the impact generated by the programme. One important study was taken up by Centre for Management Development, Thiruvanantapuram on impact assessment of the programme and found marginal improvement in income. The average annual incremental income earned by the individuals due to the assistance under the programme was Rs. 8800 whereas in case of group swarajgaris it was substantial, Rs. 34,920. It has also been observed that nearly 72 per cent of the respondents didn't undergo any training for skill development. The average cost of various individual project taken up under the programme in different states varied from Rs. 16,000 to Rs. 40,000. Nearly half of the respondents couldn't obtain second or multiple doses of credit. This apart, the Ministry of Rural Development, Government. of India has also commissioned district-wise studies across the country to know the impact of rural development programmes, including SGSY. In a study on SGSY in West Bengal Amal Mondal observed serious deficiencies with regard to the market support to the swarozogaris (Amal Mandal, 2005). Kundu (2008) observed in Bankura district that Swarnajayanti Grameen Swarozgar Yojana (SGSY) helped the rural poor to reduce their poverty but still failed to reduce their vulnerability. Nirmala Banerjee and Jayanti Sen (2003) in their study conducted on the working of the SGSY scheme in West Bengal found that the funding pattern is opaque and there is lack of coordination among different stakeholders. Tekkekara, T.F. (2008) found in Amaravati District, Maharashtra that the swarozgaris being formed into Self Help Groups solely with the objective of availing subsidy under the programme and bank loans were arranged even while they had not acquired the threshold level of entrepreneurial capacity and confidence to take-up self-employment project. She made a strong plea that the programme must be delinked from BPL list and the subsidy must be withdrawn. According to her the whole process of selection of beneficiary proceeds from a premise of suspicion rather of trust. With the help of field data collected in Maharashtra she further found that the assumption on investment levels necessary for poverty alleviation under SGSY are unrealistic.

The Comptroller and Auditor General (CAG Report on SGSY, 2003) have observed that all over the country the programme couldn't be implemented in the desired manner. It felt that the implementing agencies didn't carry out the required planning and didn't prepare the swarozgaris for taking up self-employment. In fact although the programme was conceived on process oriented one, the activities—such as proper identification of swarozjgaris, selection of key activities, market survey, networking the swarozjgaris were not carried out properly in many districts. The report even went to the extent of saying that SGSY has not emerged as an improvement over the earlier IRDP.

National Institute of Rural Development, Hyderabad conducted a National Study on SGSY during 2006. The study was taken up with the principal objective of providing detailed insight into the planning process and identifying constraints in the implementation process. The study found a positive relationship between incremental employment and incremental income suggesting marginal productivity of labour in trades like vegetable and fruit vending, spices manufacturing and handicrafts. The average post-project income of the SGSY group swarozjgaris was Rs. 1356, at least 46 per cent less than the level of income desired in the project objectives.

Though several aspects of SGSY have already been studied, but there is dearth of studies regarding participation decision of the household in the programme, and targeting efficiency of the programme. The article is organized as follows. Section III discusses data and methodology. Section IV finds determinants of SGSY participation and Section V deals with targeting efficiency aspect of SGSY programme.

Section III: Data and Methodology

Sampling Scheme

The District of Murshidabad, West Bengal, has been chosen as the field of study. In the District of Murshidabad, there are 5 SDs, 26 Blocks, 256 GPs and 2290 Mouzas. In order to grasp the ecological variation in the study we have chosen Kandi Sub-Division, part of 'Rarh Bengal', and Berhampore Sub-Division, part of 'Barendra Bengal'. The households are sampled in villages that are with and without the SGSY programme. In programme villages both the programme participants and non-participants are sampled. The sampling was done from the detailed list of SHGs provided by the District Rural Development Cell (DRDC). At the stage of sampling of SHGs under SGSY scheme, however, an intervening stratification by categories of socio-religious communities was introduced. SHGs were classified among four strata by caste and community affiliation: Scheduled Caste Hindus (SCs), Other Backward Castes (OBCs), Muslims and Upper castes (UCs). Here Muslim means Muslim General Caste. Thirty Groups, each having two and half year's age, were chosen from each Sub-Division. Five members from each group were chosen randomly and interviewed. Each group consists of 10 to 15 members. Therefore, total three hundred SHG members were interviewed. Seventy individuals having same socio-economic background as SHG members' from the programme villages of each region were interviewed. Similarly thirty individuals from the non-programme villages of each Sub-Division were interviewed. Initially it was done in 2006. The survey started from January and ended in July to minimize recall period about their pre- SHG participation socio-economic situation. As all the SHGs are two years old, therefore, pre-SHG year implies 2004. In 2006 the sample contains hundred twenty Muslim SHG members and sixty SHG members were interviewed for each of the other three SRCs. All these individuals were resurveyed in 2008. During this period twenty-three SHG members have left the group, whereas 8 individuals who were non-SHG members became SHG members in programme villages in 2008. Therefore, in 2008 we have 277 individuals who are SHG members and 132 individuals who are non-SHG members in programme villages and sixty non-SHG members from non-programme villages. Therefore, in 2008 among 277 SHG members 109 are Muslims, 58 are UCs, 55 are OBCs and 55 are SCs. Among 132 non-SHG members of programme villages 55 are Muslims, 29 are UCs, 30 are OBCs and 28 are SCs. Among 60 non-SHG members of non-programme villages 30 are Muslims and other three SRCs each have 10 members. Programme villages in Kandi Sub-Division are Salar, Raigram.

As participation in SGSY is a binary variable, therefore, determinants of participation will be assessed through 'Binary Logit regression'.

Section IV: Determinants of SGSY Participation

Several socio-economic factors determine participation of an individual in SGSY programme. The participation rule followed by an individual is specified in equation (1) where the decision to participate, P_i, by an individual is specified as a function of

$$P_i = f(X_i, Z_i, Y_i, R_i,) \qquad \ldots (1)$$

P_i is a binary variable. If any member of the ith household joins or forms group in the base line time period under SGSY programme then P_i takes value 1 otherwise zero (for the non-member households). X_i is a vector of social networking, Y_i describes the variables of social intermediation and Y_i stands for control variables. Control variable gathers information regarding household. R_i is index of perceived riskiness of repayment failure. A linear specification of equation (1) would be:

$$P_i = \alpha + \beta X_i + \gamma Z_i \, \delta Y_i + \mu R_i + e_i \qquad \ldots (2)$$

As Sharma and Zeller (1999) rightly point out that it is in principle very difficult to identify all the explanatory variables separately. In equation 2 it is very difficult to find variables that will affect social intermediation but not perceived riskiness of repayment failure or social networking. It would be more practical to treat coefficients of *X Z Y R* to be common and represented by the vector W_i, as:

$$P_i = \alpha + \sum vWi + e \qquad \ldots (3)$$

Where is n the combined effects of four determinants of SGSY participation. *A priori* expectations on the sign of *v* are difficult to assume unless $\beta\gamma\partial\mu$ are of the same sign. It is possible, however, to make inferences based on the signs of the estimated coefficients on the relative strength of some subset of variables.

W_i contains following variables:

Number of years living in the same locality: We postulate that the members of a locality know each other better and develop social ties with the passage of time. As groups are formed among homogeneous borrowers i.e. safe borrowers form group with safe borrowers and unsafe borrowers with unsafe borrowers, therefore it is expected that long habitation in locality enhances the probability of participation in the programme.

Index of women's access to public offices and processes of political activities[1]*:* Women's access to public offices and processes of political activities imply casting vote at own will, attending Gram Sansad meeting, whether know about the legal rights of the women and different Government Programmes and schemes going on at their locality, participation in political campaign. Therefore, as the index of Individual's access to public offices and processes of political activities increases likelihood of participating in the SGSY also increase.

Index of household social capital[2]: Household social capital is computed as involvement of the household members in different organizations like Village Education Committee (VEC), Water Users Associations, Puja Committee, Local Clubs and political parties. *A priori* expectation is positive between participation in SGSY and index of Household Social Capital.

Presence of NGOs: NGOs play an active role in encouraging women to join the SHG. They organize workshop and different training programme at different Panchayati Raj Institution (PRI[3]) bodies. It is expected that presence of NGO in the village will enhance the chance of participation in SGSY:

Index of functioning of PRI[4]: An active PRI can motivate rural women to join the SHG. Functioning of PRI depends on aspects like number of meeting of the 'Gram Sansad' in each six months, initiation of National Rural Employment Guarantee Programme (NREG), availability of drinking water, organization of workshop for SHGs and what percentage of villagers use sanitary toilet.

It is expected that in better managed PRI chance of joining SGSY is higher.

Access to health facilities: Among idiosyncratic risk, health hazard is the dominant problem. This is one of the prime reasons for repayment failure. Access to health has been described by number of sub-health centre and or primary health centre within one kilometre radius of the village. It is treated here as dummy variable. We postulate a positive relationship between access to health and SGSY participation.

Access to Market: Number of markets within one kilometre radius of the village has been taken as the proxy of access to market. Access to market opens more avenues of income generation. Our *a priori* expectation is positive between access to market and SGSY participation.

Education Level: Mean education level of the adult women has been taken as the explanatory variable. Here education level of the prospective participant is considered and that is expressed as number of years in school. Here we expect a positive relationship between education level and SGSY participation.

Education Level[2]: Here we take square value of education to see whether there exists any non-linear relationship between education level and likelihood of joining SGSY.

Religious Status: In our study, respondent can be stratified in four Socio Religious Communities (SRCs), viz. Upper Caste Hindus (UCs), Other Backward Castes (OBCs), Scheduled Castes (SCs) and Muslims. Here Muslims mean General caste. It is expected that compared to the reference category other SRCs would have higher chance of participating in the SGSY.

Wealth status of the household[5]: It is expected that with higher level of wealth there will be greater probability of SGSY participation.

Wealth[2]: Square value of the wealth has been taken as independent variable to see whether there exists any non-linear relationship between wealth and likelihood of SGSY participation.

Gender of the Household head: It is expected that women headed household have high probability of participating the SGSY programme. It is here treated as dummy variable and take the value 1 if the household of the prospective member is woman.

Occupation of the household head: We postulate that if the occupation of the household head is non-agriculture then there is greater likelihood to participate in SGSY programme.

Index of perceived riskiness of repayment failure[6]: This index has been constructed on the basis of respondent's answer in aspects like: (a) incidence of idiosyncratic shocks, health hazards, death of the family members etc.; (b) Covariate shocks, drought, cyclone flood etc., in last two years; (c) number of repayment failure to money lender and bank; and (d) number of dependent family members in the house-hold.

Result and Discussions

A summary of the variables and estimated logit equation is given in Table1.

'Number of years living in the same locality' has no significant impact on the decision of participation, but 'Access to public offices and involvement in political process' have strong and significant positive impact. Higher value in this sphere can motivate a woman to join in SGSY. 'Social capitals of the households' also have a statistically positive significance on the participation variable. Presence of NGO, access to market both is significant. Years of schooling has significant

Table 1: Factors determine Household Participation in SGSY

Sl. No.	*Variables*	*B*	*Standard Errors*	*E(B)*
1.	Number of years living in the locality	.0551	.3885	1.0522
2.	Index of Women's access to public offices	.3585**	.1691	1.2442
3.	Index of Social capital of the households	.3217**	.1438	1.4221
4.	Presence of NGO (Ref. No.)	.1328*	.0479	1.7376
5.	Index of Functioning of PRI	.331**	.1352	1.361
6.	Access to Health	.0726	.0513	1.018
7.	Access to market (Ref. No.)	.2588**	.115	1.2897
8.1	Years of Schooling	.1491*	.0549	1.1619
8.2	Years of Schooling	-.3028*	.06	.7291
9.	SRC (Ref. Muslim)			
9.1	UC	.0828	.0552	1.0831
9.2	OBC	.2658*	.0632	1.3048
9.3	SC	.1446*	.0486	1.1463
10.1	Wealth	.7324**	.3488	1.6419
10.2	Wealth	-.8773*	.2816	.8127
11	Gender of the household head	.0392	.0429	1.041
12.	Occupation of the household head—Non-Agl. (Ref. Agl)	.1484	.0561	1.1518
13.	Index of perceived riskiness of repayment failure	-.327*	.04	.9671
14.	Constant	.4753	.6853	1.6230

Cox and Snell R square 0.554, Nagelkarke $R^2 = 0.607$

Significance level 10 per cent, 5 per cent and 1 per cent are marked by ***, ** and *.

relationship with the likelihood of programme participation. From the table it is evident that initially with higher level of schooling chance of participating in the programme enhances, but higher education increases the opportunity cost of time. Therefore, better educated people do not assess the programme much worthwhile. Therefore, education level and SGSY participation has inverted U-shaped relationship. The trend is alike for household wealth also. There also we find an inverted U shaped relationship between wealth level and the chance of programme participation.

Among SRCs UCs have less likelihood of participating SGSY programme compared to reference category, but SCs and OBCs have significant likelihood of joining SGSY. Gender of the household head and occupation of the household head don't have any significant impact of SGSY participation. Index of perceived riskiness of repayment failure has very strong negative influence on the participation in SGSY

Section V: Targeting Efficiency

Efficacy of safety net programmes depends on targeting the desired beneficiaries. The scheme was designed to provide economic asset to poor families so that they can generate income on a sustained basis and cross poverty line. Generally all members of the group should belong to families below the poverty line. However, if necessary, a maximum of 20 per cent and in exceptional cases, where essentially required, up to a maximum of 30 per cent of the members in a group may be taken from families marginally above the poverty line living contiguously with BPL families and if they are acceptable to the BPL members of the group. This will help the families of occupational groups like agricultural labourers, marginal farmers and artisans marginally above the poverty line, or who may have been excluded from the BPL list to become members of the Self-Help Group.

Most of the targeted poverty programmes in our country has not been able to deliver the desired level of outcome. Only a small fraction of the resources allotted in these schemes reach the poor due to inefficient delivery mechanism, i.e. targeting inefficiency, leakages, participation cost and large administrative cost. Targeting error arise due to exclusion of eligible household as well as inclusion of ineligible household. The first one is known as Type-I[7] error and the last one is known as Type-II[8] error. Here we have classified the entire respondents as accordingly belonging to the 'extremely poor', 'marginal', 'vulnerable', 'middle income' and 'high income' groups if the Monthly Per Capita Expenditure (MPCE) of their household was below a specified limit. In classifying the respondents in terms of poverty status I have followed the methodology used by Sengupta *et al.* (2008)[9].

Table 2: Percentage of SGSY beneficiaries by poverty Status

Poverty Status	*Percentage of SGSY Beneficiaries*
Extremely Poor	0
Poor	13.4
Marginal	36.6
Vulnerable	34
Middle Income	10.5
High Income	5.5

Source: Calculated from field investigations.

From Table 2 it is evident that none of the SGSY beneficiary is from 'extremely poor' strata. Either they have excluded themselves on the assumption that they didn't have enough capability to generate income to repay the loan, or other SHG members think that inclusion of the poorer people will enhance their risk of default of loan. Only 13.4 per cent of the SGSY beneficiaries belong to poorest quintile. Most of the beneficiaries belong to 'marginal' and 'vulnerable' category. Therefore, in the survey area the SGSY programme has not been able to reach among the poorest people.

Proper identification of vulnerable people is most crucial for proper allocation of scare resources through government interventions. The actual targeting instrument employed varies considerably across programmes. Targeting is further complicated in that many programmes use a combination of targeting instruments. For instance, while SGSY schemes are primarily meant to benefit BPL cardholders, minimum participation by STs/SCs and women are further specified (Ajwad, 2007). Table 3 shows about 10 per cent of the swarozjgaris of the 'poor' strata don't have BPL card, whereas 54.5 per cent of the 'high income' swarozjgaris have BPL cards. SGSY programme earmarked certain provisions so that richer people can't push poor at the periphery and corner the lion's share of the benefits which are meant to poor. From Table 3 it is revealed that in survey area the SGSY programme has not been able to target the beneficiaries efficiently. It suffers from both Type-I and Type-II error.

Conclusion

This paper has tried to add to the SGSY programme evaluation literature in two key areas. It is evident from our analysis that there

Table 3: Percentage of SGSY beneficiaries having different ration cards

Poverty Status / Nature of Ration card	APL	BPL	No Card
Poor	10.3	72.4	17.3
Marginal	17.9	67.9	14.2
Vulnerable	23.6	62.6	13.8
Middle Income	18.3	66.8	14.9
High Income	25.6	54.5	19.9

Source: Calculated from field investigations.

exists an inverted *U* relationship between wealth of the household and likelihood of programme participation. This inverted U relation is also true for 'years of schooling' and programme participation. It is also revealed that the programme suffers from both Type-I and Type-II errors. It implies that the programme has excluded the eligible beneficiaries and included the ineligible beneficiaries. Future studies in this area may use more data and better proxies for targeting efficiency.

NOTES

1. Index of women access to public offices and political process has been constructed on the basis of five questions. For each positive response the respondent will get one and for each negative response the respondent will get zero in the 0-5 scale. The total square will be divided by 5.
2. Here also index is based on five questions. One point is obtained for each 'yes' and zero otherwise. Each question has equal weight. Total score will be divided by 5.
3. Panchayati Raj Institution has three tires: Gram Panchayat, the lowest tire, Panchayat Samitiy, the second tire and Zilla Parishad, the highest tire.
4. This index is based on five questions. For questions like number of meeting of the 'Gram Sansad' in each six months and percentage of villagers using sanitary toilet, score is obtained by using the formula $\frac{\text{Observed Value Mimimum Value}}{\text{Maximum Value Mimimum Value}}$ and other three questions are binary in nature. For each positive response the respondent get 1 and for each negative response the respondent get 0. Sum of all these scores will be divided by 5.
5. Most of the programme participants are agricultural labourer, petty trader and marginal farmer. They don't have any regular flow of income. So

wealth has been taken as proxy of economic status. There is high correlation between income and wealth.

6. Here all questions have equal importance. For each question, score is obtained by the formula $\frac{\text{Observed Value Mimimum Value}}{\text{Maximum Value Mimimum Value}}$. After obtaining score for each question a simple average is taken as the value of the index.
7. SGSY programme is designed for the economic improvement of the poor through generating self-employment and social mobilization. The programme is targeted in nature, and if most of the programme participants belong to non-poor section, then the poor gets excluded. Exclusion of this eligible from the programme is called type-I error.
8. Benefits of back ended subsidy and post of president or treasurer of Self-Help Group (SHG) can be enjoyed by BPL members only, but status of a SHG member depends on what type of ration card she is holding irrespective of her actual economic status. If a non-poor member has BPL ration card, then a non-eligible person has been included in the programme. This is known as type-II error.
9. Sengupta *et al.* (2008) have classified people as 'extremely poor', 'marginal', 'vulnerable', 'middle income' and 'high income' groups if the monthly per capita consumption expenditures (MPCEs) are less than or equal to Rs. 269, Rs. 348, Rs. 438, Rs. 609, Rs.1098, and Rs. 2776 respectively. This categorization is based on the data set available from the surveys of National Sample Survey Organization on employment-unemployment and consumption expenditure in 2004-05. The poverty lines as applicable to data set available from the Employment Unemployment Survey (EUS) turn out to be Rs. 346.2 for rural areas. But to get parity with the estimate of poverty line from Consumer Expenditure Survey (CES) some adjustments were also made to the estimate of poverty line from EUS. The adjusted poverty line becomes Rs. 348 per capita consumption expenditure per month. Classification of people among different economic classes is based on some specified multiple of this poverty line.

REFERENCES

1. Aghion, B. and J. Morduch (2005): *The Economics of Micro Finance*, MIT Press.
2. Banerjee, Nirmala and Joyanti Sen (2003): 'Swarnajayanti Gram Swarozgar Yojana: A Budgetary Policy in Working', New Delhi, United Nations Development Fund for Women.
3. Besley, T. and S. Coate (1995): "Group Lending, Repayment Incentives, and Social Collateral", *Journal of Development Economics*, 109(2):491-515.
4. CAG (2003): *Report on SGSY*. New Delhi. Comptroller and Auditor General of India.

5. Jain, S. and G. Mansuri (2003): "A Little at a Time: The Use of Regularly Scheduled Repayments in Micro Finance Programmes", *Journal of Development Economics*, Vol. 72, pp. 253-79
6. Kundu, A. (2008): "Impact of SGSY Scheme on Self-Help Group Members in West Bengal", *Afro Asian Journal of Rural Development.*
7. Laffont, J. and P. Rey (2003): "Collusion and Group Lending With Moral Hazard", *Working Paper*.
8. Morduch, J. (1998): "Does Micro Finance Really Help Poor? *New Evidence from Flagship Programmes in Bangladesh"*, McArthur Network Working Paper.
9. Mukherjee, A.K. and A. Kundu (2008): "Simultaneous Financing, Symmetric Group Lending and Peer Monitoring in Government Subsidized Micro Credit Programme". *Artha Beekshan,* 17(3):37-52
10. Mukherjee, A.K. and A. Kundu (2009): "Accessibility of Credit to the Rural Poor Through Reduction of Transaction Cost". In Lazar and Deo (ed.) '*Micro Finance Performance Evaluation and Enterprise Development'*, Allied Publishers, Chennai, India, p. 59-74.
11. NIRD (2006): *National Study on SGSY: A Process Study*. Hyderabad: National Institute of Rural Development.
12. Pitt, M. and S. Khandker (1998): "The Impact of Group Based Credit Programmes on Poor Households in Bangladesh: Does the Gender of the Participants Matter?", *Journal of Political Economy,* 106(5):961-996.
13. Sengupta, A., K.P. Kanan and G. Ravendran, 2008, "India's Common People: Who Are They, How Many Are They and How Do They Live?", *Economic and Political Weekly*, Vol. XLIII, No. 11, pp. 49-63.
14. Sharma, M. and M. Zeller (1999): "Placement and Outreach of Group Based Credit Organizations: The Case of ASA, BRAC, and Proshika in Bangladesh", *World Development,* 27(12):2123-2136.
15. Stiglitz, J. (1990):"Peer Monitoring and Credit markets", *World Bank Economic Review*, 4(3):351-366.
16. Thekkekara, T.F. (2008): 'Impact of SGSY on SHG: Bank Linkage' in *Micro Finance* Edited by K.G. Karmakar, Sage Publications, Delhi, pp.188-214.

8

National Agricultural Insurance Scheme: A Study of Some Selected Districts of West Bengal

Arabinda Ghosh

1. Introduction

Since the beginning of the plan period in our country the share of agriculture in GDP has been declining without any matching decline in occupational distribution in favour of agriculture. An NSSO survey among 51,770 farmers in 6638 villages spreading over the country in 2005-06 shows that annual average farm income of a farmer is Rs. 11,628 and annual average farm expenditure is Rs. 8,791. Thus a very low annual net income of Rs. 2,837 cannot but lead a farmer to indebtedness even if they are resorting to various non-farm occupations. Although their problem of indebtedness has been well acknowledged, a democratic society cannot ignore equity and justice. In a growing society ensuring food security, adoption of progressive farming practices, diversification of crops in favour riskier but higher value crops, stabilizing farm incomes are truly urgent. Introduction of crop insurance scheme is, indeed, a humble beginning in this direction. Different forms of experiments for about 30 years gave birth to National Agricultural Insurance Scheme (NAIS) from 'rabi' season of 1999-2000. But the multi-dimensionality and the complex nature of the scheme prevent it from gaining popularity.

Although we find a few works on the need for introduction of agricultural insurance, but systematic study related to the progress and problems of agricultural insurance in India is truly negligible in the literature. Kalavakonda and Mahul (2005) studied the progress of 'NAIS' in Karnataka on the basis of a survey of 100 households in 2003 at the initiative of Karnataka Government. They found that the coverage of the scheme is limited to only 16 per cent of the state's farmers and the claim-premium ratio, equal to 7, is very high. Vyas and Singh (2006) made a comprehensive review of NAIS on the basis of a detailed analysis of exhaustive data for 11 crop seasons covering from 'rabi' of 1999-2000 to 'rabi' of 2004-05. Their study was based on field investigations in the states of Haryana, Rajasthan, Andhra Pradesh, Madhya Pradesh and Gujarat. The authors gave their observations on issues like determination of premium rates, determination of threshold yield, role of different stakeholders and above all, the role of Agricultural Insurance Corporation of India Ltd. (AICI). Raju and Chand (2007) reviewed the progress of NAIS till 2004-05. They argued that for the scheme to be viable premium rates should be reasonably revised, private insurance companies should be involved and there is need to cover market risk.

But the study related to the progress of various crop insurance schemes, including NAIS, is really lacking in the context of West Bengal. This paper has made a preliminary attempt to throw some light on the progress of NAIS in two districts of West Bengal, viz. Hooghly and Purulia. Our study gives some interesting picture which would certainly help to get a view of the progress and drawbacks of NAIS. This paper also attempts to make some recommendations in the light of experience gathered from the study for the improvement of the agricultural insurance programme in the country.

This paper is organized in the following manner. Section 2 analyses a brief history of agricultural insurance in India with a close look on NAIS. Section 3 gives the methodology, result and analysis of the study. Finally concluding remarks are made in Section 4.

2. A Brief History of Agricultural Insurance in India

Different forms of experiments on agricultural insurance on a limited, *ad hoc* and scattered scale started from 1972-73. The first such scheme was introduced by GIC and it covered H-4 cotton, groundnut, wheat and potato. It was implemented in Andhra Pradesh, Gujarat, Karnataka, Maharashtra, Tamil Nadu and West Bengal. The scheme continued up to 1978-79 and 3,110 farmers came under it with a premium of Rs. 4.54 lakh against claims of Rs. 37.88 lakh.

In 1976 Prof. V.M. Dandekar was entrusted to conduct a study on the scheme. On the basis of his recommendations, a Pilot Crop Insurance Scheme (PCIS) was launched by the GIC in 1979. It was based on "area approach" rather than "individual approach" of the previous scheme for providing insurance cover against a decline in crop yield below the threshold yield. The scheme covered cereals, millets, oilseeds, cotton and potato and it was confined to loanee farmers, taking loans from institutional sources, on voluntary basis. The risk was shared by GIC and State Governments on 2:1 basis. The maximum sum insured was equivalent to crop loan with premium ranged from 5 to 10 per cent of the sum insured. Till 1984-85, it was implemented in 13 states and covered 6.27 lakh farmers for a premium of Rs. 196.95 lakh against claims of Rs. 157.05 lakh.

In 1985 Comprehensive Crop Insurance Scheme (CCIS) replaced PCIS with minor modifications to cover only loanee farmers on compulsory basis. Premium rates were reduced with 50 per cent subsidy to small and marginal farmers. The burden of premium and claims was shared by the Central and State Governments on 2:1 basis. Fifteen States and two Union Territories (UTs) join the scheme. Till 1999-2000, 763 lakh farmers were covered with a premium of Rs. 404 crore. against claims of Rs. 2303 crore. While CCIS was being implemented a new scheme, Experimental Crop Insurance Scheme (ECIS), was launched in 'rabi' of 1997-98 in 14 districts of 5 states. It covers only small and marginal farmers with 100 per cent subsidy in premium. But, due to some difficulties, it was discontinued after one season. Again CCIS was abandoned and a new scheme in the name of NAIS was introduced.

National Agricultural Insurance Scheme (NAIS)

Under the supervision of AICI, NAIS was introduced from 'rabi' season of 1999-2000. The main objectives of the scheme are:

(i) to provide insurance coverage and financial support to all farmers in the event of failure of any notified crop in notified areas as a result of natural calamities, pests and diseases;
(ii) to restore the credit eligibility of farmers, after a crop failure, for the next season;

(iii) to encourage farmers to adopt progressive farming practices, high value inputs and higher technology in agriculture; and
(iv) to help stabilize farm incomes, particularly in disaster years.

The scheme covers all foodgrains, oilseeds and annual horticultural and commercial crops like sugarcane, potato, cotton, jute, banana, pineapple, etc. The scheme is based on both 'area approach' for widespread calamities and 'individual approach' for localized calamities such as hailstorms, landslides, cyclones and floods. The scheme is both voluntary and compulsory in nature. It is voluntary in two senses: (a) States/UTs enjoy the freedom of joining the scheme, as Punjab and some North-Eastern states do not join it. The states are also free to choose specific crops and areas to be covered in a particular agricultural season; and (b) non-loanee farmers may or may not purchase a particular insurance product. But the scheme is compulsory for all loanee farmers in notified areas and for notified crops.

The premium rates for food crops varies from 1.5 per cent to 3.5 per cent of the sum insured, depending on the crop and season; and for horticultural/commercial crops, the actuarial rates apply. AICI also revises these rates from time to time. For example, the premium rate for potato was Rs. 2.88 in 2006-07 but raised to Rs. 3.56 in 2007-08. A subsidy of 50 per cent on premiums of small and marginal farmers was equally shared by the Central and State Governments and it was proposed to be phased out within 5 years. The sum insured is equal to the loan amount, but it can be extended up to a value of 150 per cent of average yield. For non-loanee farmers the insurable amount can also be of 150 per cent of average yield.

The loss assessment and indemnity payment is based on the actual *yield data* obtained from States' Department of Economics and Statistics[1]. If the actual yield per hectare falls short of the *threshold yield* all the insured farmers will be eligible for indemnity payment. The threshold yield is calculated by multiplying the average yield with the indemnity level. Average yield is obtained by the moving average of last 3 years yield for rice and wheat and last 5 years yield for other crops. Indemnity level varies from 60 per cent to 90 per cent depending on the nature of risk of the crop.

Thus, *threshold yield or guaranteed yield* = *Average yield* × *Indemnity level.*

The claim settlement process is somewhat cumbersome. A number of agencies are involved in this process. AICI is the implementing agency. Claim settlements are based on instruction from AICI.

Claim amount = (Shortfall in actual yield/Threshold yield) × Insured Amount.

The funds needed to pay claims beyond the risk sharing limits of AICI are provided by both Central and State Governments on equal sharing basis.

Upto the 'rabi season of 2006-07 the scheme has been introduced in 23 States and 2 UTs. In the country as a whole it covers 970.73 lakh farmers with a premium of Rs. 2942.71 crore. and claims payment of Rs. 9373.24 cr. to 270 lakh farmers. In the same period in West Bengal it covered 50.78 lakh farmers with premium of Rs. 96.37 crore. against claims payment of Rs. 158.76 crore to 107 lakh farmers. During this period NAIS has reached to only 15 per cent of the country's farmers, 16 per cent of the total farmed area and 4 per cent of value of crop output. Of the total number of farmers covered in India 79.51 per cent are loanee. Thus 20.49 per cent of non-loanee farmers are covered by the scheme. Unfortunately, no non-loanee farmer is covered in West Bengal. From 'rabi', 2006-07 to 'kharif', 2009, the scheme covered 552.80 lakh farmers with a premium of Rs. 2323 crore and claims payment of Rs. 9352 crore. to 148 lakh farmers in the country as a whole. The performance of different insurance schemes introduced in India is summarized in Table 1.

3. Methodology, Result and Analysis of the Study

The two districts, Hooghly and Purulia, chosen for the study of the progress of NAIS in West Bengal are different in terms of geographical location and agricultural advancement. The former is situated in Gangetic planes but the latter is located in Chotanagpur plateau. Most of the farmed areas in Hooghly are irrigated and there are provisions for double cropping and multiple cropping. But, almost the entire district of Purulia is rainfed, non-irrigated and single cropped. The opportunity and scope of non-farm occupations are also greater in Hooghly. Some important features of these districts could be found from Table 2 and Table 3.

Table 1: Progress of Different Agricultural Insurance Schemes in India

Name of the Insurance Scheme	*Period Covered*	*No. of Farmers Covered*	*Premium Collected (in Rs.)*	*Claims Paid (in Rs)*	*Claim-Premium Ratio*
First Individual Approach Scheme	1972-73 to 1978-79	3,110	4.54 lakh	37.88 lakh	8.34
PCIS	1979-80 to 1984-85	6.27 lakh	196.95 lakh	157.05 lakh	0.79
CCIS	1985-86 to 1998-99	763 lakh	404 cr.	2303 cr.	5.70
NAIS	1999-2000 to 2006-07	970.73 lakh	2943 cr.	9373 cr.	3.18
NAIS	2006-07 to Khariff, 2009	552.80 lakh	2323 cr.	9352 cr.	4.02

Source: AICI Report.

Table 2: Some basic features of Hooghly and Purulia Districts

District	*No. of Block*	*No. of GP*	*No. of Village*	*Total Cropped Area (in thousand hectares)*	*Irrigated Area (in Percentage)*	*Annual Average Rainfall (in mm.)*
Hooghly	18	210	1886	225.17	61	1129
Purulia	20	170	2468	339.14	19	1260

Source: Bureau of Applied Statistics and Economics, Government of West Bengal.

Table 3: Pattern of Land Holding in Hooghly and Purulia

District	*Marginal*	*Small*	*Medium and Large*	*Total*	*Average Size of Holding*
Hooghly	284330	38309	9454	332008	0.66 ha.
Purulia	213085	63750	24679	301514	0.86 ha.

Source: Bureau of Applied Statistics and Economics, Government of West Bengal

The data for the purpose of this study are collected with the help of stratified sampling method. On the basis of some criteria, like number. of bargadars, number. of small and marginal farmers, net area sown and net area sown with more than one crop grown, etc., three blocks for each of the district are chosen. In the second stage, at first one Gram Panchayat (G.P.) in each block and then two villages from each G.P. are selected. In the third and final stage some farmers are chosen in each village for interaction so that each category of farmer is adequately represented. The interaction with the farmers has been made on the basis of a set of questionnaire.

In Purulia fifty farmers have been interviewed, forty three of them are either small and marginal farmers or bargadars. The annual average farm and non-farm income of these farmers during last five years is about Rs. 30,000. The number of loanee farmers was 24 (48 per cent of the farmers) of which 9 (37 per cent of the loanee farmers) farmers got loans from institutional sources. None of them has ever heard of any crop insurance scheme and nor they have received any such claims as compensation for crop loss. The farmers who took loans from institutional sources were not aware (with one exception only) of whether any premium is deducted from their crop loans. Interestingly, all the farmers are eager to join the scheme but they admit their helplessness in getting institutional loan. Most surprisingly, no gram panchayat member, so far interacted by the author, knows about the existence of such scheme. Even district head office of the agricultural department does not have any record about the progress of NAIS in the district.

But, in Hooghly, NAIS has been able to make some inroads among farmers. Twenty farmers have been interviewed. Their annual average farm income is about Rs. 50,000 and annual average farm expenditure is about Rs. 40,000. The number of loanee farmers was 14 (about 70 per cent) and among them about 60 per cent took loans from institutional sources. Some of them received insurance claims twice in last six years:- in 'rabi' 2002-03 and in 'rabi' 2004-05. In 2006-07, although announcement for claims payable for the crop loss in potato has been made, farmers have not yet received it. In 2004-05, the scheme covered 37,062 farmers (about 11 per cent of farmers of the district) and 3.7 per cent of cropped area with a premium of Rs. 1.15 crore. against claims of Rs. 7.07 crore in the district. The sincerity of the district authority for the implementation of NAIS is evident as an employee has been specially recruited to monitor the scheme.

The dismal performance of Purulia district *vis-à-vis* Hooghly can be attributed to some valid arguments. Farmers of Purulia do not grow 'potato', usually on commercial basis, which is considered to be a major commercial crop in Hooghly. Cultivation of this particular crop needs huge investment and it also involves a greater degree of risk. Consequently, farmers of Hooghly are heavily inclined to get access to institutional loans and to get compulsorily insured. Farming in Purulia is still monsoon based and farmers rely on traditional methods requiring less fertilizers, less pesticides and above all, less investment. The demand as well as access to institutional loans is relatively less there. Though institutional loans are necessarily insured, but loss of crops as compared to relatively low annual average yield of last three years is somehow remain neglected and unnoticed in Purulia. Secondly, lack of awareness among farmers, particularly, among people's representatives about the scheme hampers the progress of NAIS in Purulia. In Hooghly, when farmers suffer crop loss, particularly, in potato farming, they put pressures on people's representatives and also on credit institutions, especially on Primary Agricultural Credit Societies to get insurance claims. Evidences prove that such pressure tactics sometimes yield favourable result. Thirdly, lack of motivation among government officials to implement the scheme in Purulia is prominent. When this author once contacted District Director of NABARD about the inclusion of non-loanee farmers his advice was contrary to the progress of the scheme.

The preliminary study discloses some serious drawbacks of the scheme and these drawbacks could be found in other districts of the state and other states as well. Firstly, the insurance scheme could not cover any non-loanee farmer of these districts. Till 2004-05, about 20 per cent of the farmers covered under the scheme in India are non-loanee, but no progress in this regard has taken place in West Bengal. In fact, the scheme is too critical for a non-loanee farmer to join it. In order to insure the crops, at first, a non-loanee farmer is to obtain certificate from the local agricultural officer regarding the nature of crop and area cultivated. Then the farmer is to deposit the premium[2] along with the certificate in the designated insurance office of the district. So, one cannot expect such clumsy process to be followed by a common farmer to insure the crops.

Secondly, as the scheme is compulsory for loanee farmers, unless the scope of institutional loan is extended, it is difficult for a larger section of farmers to come under its purview. The study in the two districts of West Bengal shows that due to non-cooperative attitude of some banks, particularly commercial banks, lack of security/ collateral requirement of small and marginal farmers and lack of adequate connection/information farmers are deprived of institutional loans. There is a deadline as notified by the AICI and the concerned State Government within which crop loan is to be disbursed for getting insurance coverage. Financial institutions[3] are not very serious about maintaining this deadline. Thus unfortunate farmers are deprived of the benefit of being insured.

Thirdly, because of the involvement of different agencies, it takes a long time to settle the claims when crop loss is established. About 10 to 15 different governmental departments are engaged in this process. The delay in claim settlement frustrates the credit eligibility of the farmers for the next season. We could see it from the experience of potato farmers of Hooghly district in 2006-07. Although claims have been announced, yet farmers did not receive it till February 2008.

Fourthly, the programme of NAIS has been suffering from very high claim-premium ratio. The average claim-premium ratio for the country as a whole is 3.18 up to 2006-07, but sometimes it becomes very high as we see that during rabi season of 2004-05 it was 6.14 in Hooghly district. As claims exceeded premiums by a large margin, the scheme suffers from a net loss even if administrative costs are excluded.

Fifthly, NAIS does not cover any market risk. Sometimes, the yield is good, but due to bumper production of crops market prices fall to unremunerative level. Thus farmers suffer income loss due to distress selling. Since NAIS covers risk against yield failure farmers are not entitled to get any claim as compensation. Recently, AICI introduced 'Farm Income Insurance Scheme' from rabi season of 2003-04 in order to cover the market risk. But it was introduced only for rice and wheat in 20 districts of the country of which the district of Burdwan from West Bengal was one.

Sixthly, the choice or the selection of the unit area for covering risk, in some cases, puts extra burden on claims payment for compensating those who do not actually suffer any crop loss and in some cases fails to compensate those who are the real victims. Since the unit area in the "area approach" scheme is either a block or a gram panchayat some parts of the area may not be affected, yet farmers of those parts are entitled to get claims. Again, some parts of the adjoining block/gram panchayat may genuinely suffer crop loss but farmers do not receive any claim as the adjacent block has not been declared eligible to get insurance coverage on the basis of crop-cutting experiment.

4. Concluding Remarks

There is no denying fact that introduction of crop insurance scheme has been a major breakthrough in the development of the agrarian sector of the economy, but different programmes of crop insurance schemes have not done enough to fulfil the objectives of agricultural insurance. There is still widespread indebtedness[4] among farmers. There were almost 10,000 incidents of suicides[5] by farmers between 2001 and 2006. Inequality in income between rural and urban households and also between cultivators and non-cultivators among rural households is alarming. The motivation to switchover to non-farm activities has been strengthening since early 1990s.

AICI has set a target to reach 40 per cent of the nation's farmers by 2010. In order to achieve this target it should thoroughly review NAIS to make suitable changes in it. As the scheme is compulsory for loanee farmers adequate arrangements need to be made to include more and more farmers under the umbrella of institutional loans. It should be ensured that farmers from all sections of the society including small and marginal farmers, bargadars, SCs, STs, minorities get access to the loans. At the same time, farmers should be encouraged to build regular repayment habits so that banks do not lose focus on agricultural lending. Reluctance of commercial banks could be minimized by strict observance of the RBI directive that 18 per cent of banks' loans must be directed to agriculture. Banks must also ensure compulsory coverage of the loanee farmers under NAIS by observing the deadline for loan disbursement.

Timely settlement and release of claims are regarded as the key to the success of NAIS. Usually it takes at least one year after the completion of harvesting of crops. Arrangements may be made for *ex-gratia* payments once crop loss is established so that their credit eligibility is not hampered. A fund could be created for the purpose through joint contribution from Central and State Governments. Better coordination among different departments is also required to avoid unnecessary loss of time.

In fact, the financial performance of the scheme could be improved by reducing its reliance on the Central and State Governments. One

Governments. One way of improving it is to increase premium rates on the basis of past experience of all-India claim-premium ratio. Given the value of crop output, the existing premiums are, indeed, very low. Since claim-premium ratio, at present, is 3.18, doubling or trebling the premium rates would not harm the farmers much, but it would nevertheless improve the financial performance of the scheme. Subsidy to premiums of small and marginal farmers should be discontinued and medium and large farmers may be asked to pay premiums at a higher rate. Keeping in mind of food security and priority, premiums for food crops and oilseeds should be fixed at lower levels as compared to commercial and horticultural crops. As uncertainty and vulnerability vary from state to state and also within a state, premium rates for a state/region should be so determined such that they could reflect riskiness of the region. There is an opinion that AICI could think of charging actuarial rates.

In order to cover risk against price fluctuations farm income insurance scheme, already introduced for some crops and in some regions, should be extended to those crops price fluctuations for which occur frequently. Prices of jute, sugarcane and potato generally fluctuate widely. A good yield sometimes lead to very low prices. In the present system farmers would not be eligible for claims. As the farmers suffer income loss there should be some mechanism for compensation. Market risk can be covered by requiring interested farmers to register their marketable surplus with an insurance agency or market committee at the time of sowing crops[6]. The insurance agency should offer insurance cover against a premium to include price guarantee which could be the minimum support price in some cases or the market based price from the past; and also against average farm income based on average yield and market price/minimum support price.

For the viability of crop insurance schemes government should ensure that quality of the seeds for the crops and other inputs are good. Seeds should be stored and maintained in proper way. Strict vigilance on dealers and sellers of seeds is required so that they do not sell spurious seeds and adopt unfair practices. Sometimes poor quality seeds sold in the market are the cause of crop failure. Attempts have been initiated in West Bengal to train the farmers regarding maintenance, storage and use of seeds, fertilizers and pesticides in a scientific manner. More should be done in this regard to improve irrigation facilities and drainage facilities.

The question of allowing private insurance companies and the role of agents in canvassing different crop insurance schemes is also an important issue in the context of agricultural insurance in India. Private sector insurance has been introduced in 2003-04 in the form of 'rainfall insurance'. Private insurance companies may be invited to do business in high value crops on experimental basis with some government support in the beginning which could be slowly withdrawn.

It is a challenge to the nation to design a crop insurance system that is financially viable for the government yet affordable for the farmers and maintain sustainable growth in agriculture.

NOTES

1. District office of the Bureau of Applied Economics and Statistics, Government of West Bengal calculate the actual yield on the basis of 'crop-cutting experiments'. When the unit of area is a block then at least 16 cuts, taking 8 cuts from each of 3 randomly selected gram panchayats, are taken. As the area unit has now become a gram panchayat then at least 8 cuts are required to estimate the actual yield.
2. The insurance premium rates for non-loanee farmers are generally higher than those for loanee farmers.
3. Kalavakonda & Mahul (2005) have shown that in Karnataka only 22.7 per cent of the institutional loans in 2002-03 are covered under NAIS as the remaining loans are not disbursed in due time.
4. According to NSSO report of 2005-06, 48.6 per cent farmers of the country are indebted.
5. K.C.Suri (2006).
6. Raju and Chand (2007).

REFERENCES

Bardhan, P. and Christopher Udry (1999): "Development Microeconomics", Oxford University Press, New Delhi.

Dandekar, V.M. (1976): "Crop Insurance in India", *Economic and Political Weekly, Review of Agriculture* (June 1976).

Hardekar, J.B., R.B.M. Huirne and J.R. Anderson (1997): "*Coping With Risk in Agriculture*", CAB International, New York.

Kalavakonda, Vijay and Olivier Mahul (2005): "Crop Insurance in Karnataka", *World Bank Policy Research Working Paper Series 3654.*

Ministry of Food and Agriculture (August 1971): "*Report of the Expert Committee on Crop Insurance*".

Raju, S.S. and Ramesh Chand (2007): "Progress and Problems in Agricultural Insurance", *Economic and Political Weekly*, (May 26-June 1, 2007).

Ray, Debraj (2004): "*Development Economics*", Oxford University Press, New Delhi.

Selvarajan, E. and R. Elango (2004): "*Rural Development Programmes and Externalities*", Serial Publications, New Delhi.

Suri, K.C. (2006): "Political Economy of Agrarian Distress", *Economic and Political Weekly*, April 2006).

Townsend, Robert M. (1994): "Risk and Insurance in Village India", *Econometrica*, Vol. 62/1.

Vyas, V.S. and Surjit Singh (2006): "Crop Insurance in India", *Economic and Political Weekly* (November 2006).

www.aicofindia.com: Business Reports of Agricultural Insurance Company of India Ltd.

9

Sources of Output Growth in West Bengal Agriculture: A District Level Study

Subrata Kundu

Introduction

Even after 50 years of independence, agriculture continues to be the mainstay of the Indian economy. It accounts for about one-fourth (25 per cent) of the Gross Domestic Product (GDP) and is the sources of livelihood for nearly two-third (60 per cent) of the population. The green revolution has been the cornerstone of India's agricultural achievement, transforming the country from one of food deficiency to self-sufficiency through enhanced technology adoption, increased public and private investments and creation institutional innovations that have augmented production and productivity gain.

Eastern India has emerged as a new centre of growth in the agricultural sector since the 1980s. A notable feature of the accelerated growth performance in the eighties and the early nineties is the striking performance of foodgrains, especially rice. Over this period, the food-grains production increased at a compound annual rate of 3.1 per cent per annum in this region. Of India's incremental output of 45.6 million tonnes in foodgrains over this period, around 20 per cent was contributed by the Eastern region. In West Bengal the growth rate of rice production increased to more than 6 per cent per annum. The significant upsurge in agricultural productivity in general is attributed to two major factors. One is the role of institutional changes. Studies by Mukherjee and Mukhopadhyay (1996), Ray Chaudhari and Sen

(1996), Sanyal *et al.* (1998), Rawal and Swaminathan (1998) highlight the role of Operation Barga in reversing the slow output growth in West Bengal. According to them, the establishment of the democratic panchayati institution in West Bengal and the conduct of Operation Barga were main factors behind the transition in West Bengal's agricultural performance. Operation Barga, started in 1978, involved recording the names of the sharecroppers, thereby granting them heritable rights of cultivation and minimizing the risk of eviction. Quick recording of Barga rights of and provision for institutional credit to the sharecroppers raised the access of the small operators to technological inputs.

The second factor is the wider adoption of new technology, better utilization of fertilizers credit and so on. So far, the literature on Eastern India has emphasized the role of institutional changes and relegated the role of productivity growth to be of secondary importance. This is not to suggest that institutional changes and productivity are mutually exclusive; rather institutional changes facilitate productivity; for example, by enabling technological change. Yet, quantification of productivity growth and its sources has not been attempted systematically in the literature. As to the case of West Bengal, there is an ongoing debate about the acceleration in the growth of major agricultural crops in the aftermath of the institutional changes brought about by the policy of land reforms in the eighties. While there were some studies (such as Boyce, 1987; Saha and Swaminathan, 1994), which predicted such a break, the findings of some other studies (Chattopadhyay, Neogi and Maity, 1993; Rudra, 1992) based on the same data set did not corroborate this view.

There has been a lot of debate regarding the productivity growth in West Bengal (Boyce, 1987; Saha and Swaminathan, 1994; Chattopadhyay and Das, 2000; Chattopadhyay, Neogi and Maity, 1993; Sen and Sengupta, 1995; Mukhopadhyay and Sarkar, 2001; Sawant and Achuthan, 1995; Sengupta, Bhattacharya and Chattopadhyay, 2004). While some of these studies point out to a major break in West Bengal agriculture (such as Boyce, 1987; Saha and Swaminathan, 1994), others (such as Chattopadhyay *et al.* 1993) fails to find any major break. Majority of such analysis are based primarily of simple yield growth rate[1]. Recently there has been some development in the field of productivity analysis incorporating both parametric and non-parametric approaches (such as Total Factor Productivity Growth (TFPG), Malmquist indices, Efficiency corrected productivity indices etc.). These concepts utilize both input and output data in analyzing productivity and efficiency. In this paper an attempt has been made to decompose the output growth into input growth and total factor productivity district-wise and further to decompose the TFP into technical efficiency and technological change using non-parametric approach.

This paper is divided into four Sections. In Section (2), we give a brief description of the data used. Section (3) discusses the methodology and estimation. Finally, Section (4) concludes the study.

2. Data Description

Farmers in underdeveloped areas exhibit wide differences in their resource use pattern. It thus seems interesting to study efficiency differentials among farmers of different categories and to analyze the factors that may lead to such difference in observed behaviour. In our exercise we have considered the cultivation of different crops in West Bengal. West Bengal is one of the provinces in India where large-scale land improvement policies have resulted in breaking up of vested interests in land holding pattern to a certain extent (Dyer, 1998). Several authors argued that such measures have contributed to significant efficiency gains (Banerjee, Gertler and Ghatak, 2002). It thus remains imperative to examine the extent to which these gains have been translated in production economies. In the region under study paddy is the main crop (Dyer, 1998). The crop is generally cultivated more than once a year (normally referred to as *aman, boro and aus*). Aman is the traditional variety while boro is the modern variety with high return, huge investment and large risk involved. In recent years, aus have been substituted by some other crops (such as mustard, potato, etc.). Jute is another important commercial crop that is grown in this state.

The data we have used in this exercise has been collected under the cost of cultivation scheme conducted by the Bidhan Chandra Krishi Visvavidalaya, Kalyani, Nadia, in West Bengal. The data were collected for every district of this province each year. A multistage random sampling design was adopted from blocks to mouza and then from mouza to households. The landless labourers were excluded from the set of households. We have used in this study district-level aggregate data pertaining to the years 1980-2000 for all the major districts. West Bengal exhibits wide socio-economic and geographical features.[2]

The data set supplies information on various inputs like human labour, bullock labour, fertilizer, manure, machine and output of all the crops cultivated both in value and quantitative terms. For our estimation, we have taken several inputs, namely human labour, bullock labour, fertilizer and manure, machine hour, irrigation charge, implements which presumably explain production of most of the crops very well. For output we have taken total value of all the crops, each crop being evaluated at the district level price for that crop and year[3], the time period is twenty years[4]. Information is also provided for other items of farm expenditure as well.

Methodology and Estimation

An evaluation of agricultural growth performance can be made in several ways. One important method is to identify the sources of output growth so as to gauge whether it is due to increase in inputs, increase in input use efficiency, or improvement in the existing technology or introduction of new technology. Total factor productivity which is defined as growth in output which is not explained by input growth but a combined result of technical progress and technical efficiency or the efficiency with which factors are used, given the technical progress, to produce output (Fan,1991). The existing studies on total factor productivity in Indian agriculture have not made this distinction in their analysis (Rosegrant and Evenson, 1992; Dholakia and Dholakia, 1993; Kumar and Rosegrant, 1994). At first, Kalirajan *et al.* (1997) made this distinction in their analysis. They estimated the technical efficiency in production using the stochastic production function of Cobb-Douglas type. A large number of studies are available on the use of stochastic production function for the measurement of technical efficiency in production (Farrell, 1957; Aigner *et al.*, 1977; Meeusen and Van den Broeck, 1977). Unlike the methods, Kalirajan *et al.* (1997) estimated technical change as a shift in the production frontiers distinguishing from improvement in technical efficiency and treated the total input growth as the residual. In this approach the technical progress is considered to be non-neutral.

Following figure illustrates the decomposition of total output growth into input growth, technical progress and technical efficiency improvement. In period 1 and 2 the firm faces production frontiers F_1 and F_2 respectively. If a given firm has been technically efficient, output would be y^*_1 in period 1 and y^*_2 in period 2. On the other hand, if the firm is technically inefficient and does not operate on its frontier, then the firm's realized output is y_1 in period 1 and y_2 in period 2. Technical inefficiency (TE) is measured by the vertical distances between the frontier output and the realized output of the given firm. That is, TE_1 in period 1 and TE_2 in period 2 respectively. Hence, the change in technical efficiency over time is the difference between the TE_1 and TE_2. Now suppose, there is technical progress due to the improvement quality of human and physical capital, so a firm's potential frontier shifts to F_2 in period 2. If the given firm keeps up with the technical progress, more output is produced from the same level of input. So the firm's output will be y_1^{**} from x_1 input shown in the figure. Technical progress is measured by the distance between two frontiers $(y_1^{**} - y_1^{*})$ evaluated at x_1. Denoting the contribution of input growth to output growth (between periods 1 and 2) as Δy_x, the total output growth, $(y_2 - y_1)$, can be decomposed into three components: input growth, technical progress and technical efficiency change. Referring to the figure, the decomposition can be shown as follows:

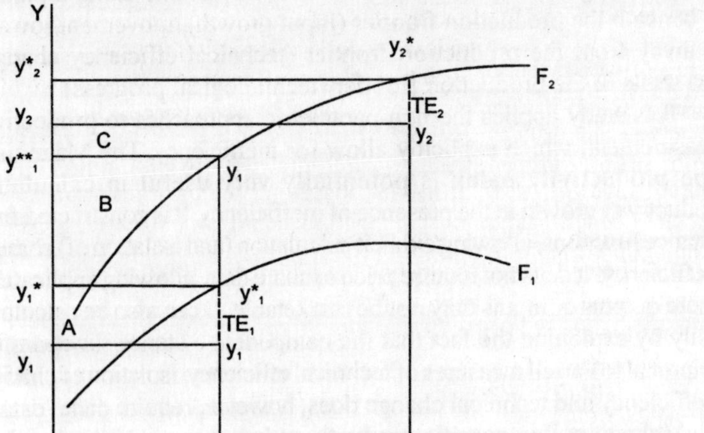

Decomposition of Output Growth

$$D = y_2 - y_1$$

$$= A + B + C$$

$$= (y_1^{*} - y_1) + (y_1^{**} - y_1^{*}) + (y_2 - y_1^{**})$$

$$= (y_1^* - y_1) + (y_1^{**} - y_1^*) + (y_2^* - y_1^{**}) - (y_2^* - y_2)$$

$$= \left[(y_1^* - y_1) - (y_2^* - y_2)\right] + (y_1^{**} - y_1^*) + (y_2 - y_1^{**})$$

$$= [TE_1 - TE_2] + TC + \Delta y_1$$

where $y_2 - y_1$ = output growth,

$TE_1 - TE_2$ = technical efficiency change,

TC = technical change,

Δy_x = output growth due to input growth.

The decomposition in the above model enriches Solow's dichotomy by attributing observed output growth to movements along a path on or beneath the production frontier (input growth), movement towards or away from the production frontier (technical efficiency change), and shifts in the production frontier (technological progress).

This study applies the non-parametric approaches to productivity measurement, which explicitly allow for inefficiency. The Malmquist-type productivity index is potentially very useful in calculating productivity growth in the presence of inefficiency. It is constructed from distance functions, allowing explicit calculation (and isolation of) changes in efficiency. It does not require price or share data, allowing applications where outputs or inputs may not be marketable. It can also be calculated easily by exploiting the fact that the component distance functions are reciprocal to Farrell measures of technical efficiency. Isolation of changes in efficiency and technical change does, however, require panel data.

Malmquist firm-specific productivity indexes were introduced by Caves, Christensen and Diewert (1982a). They named these indexes after Malmquist, who had early proposed constructing input quantity indexes as ratio of distance functions {see Malmquist (1953)}. Indeed, these Malmquist indexes are construct from ratios of distance functions, which are a natural way of modelling the production frontier as well as deviations from and shifts in that frontier, that is, technical inefficiency and technical change. Although not recognized by Caves, Christensen and Diewert at the time,[5] the formulation of these indexes in terms of distance functions also leads to straightforward calculation by exploiting the relation between distance function and Farrell measures of technical efficiency.

To define an output-based Malmquist productivity index, assume that for each time period=1, 2, 3........,T, the production technology S^t models the transformation of inputs $x^t \in R_+^N$ into outputs $y^t \in R_+^M$. It is also assumed that S^t is sufficiently regular to define meaningful output distance functions[6].

$$D_0^t\left(x^t, y^t\right)=\inf\left\{\theta:\left(x^t, y^t/\theta\right)\in S^t\right\} \qquad ...(1)$$

Note that $D_0^t(x^t, y^t) \leq 1$ if and only if $(x^t, y^t) \in S^t$. It follows from the definition of the distance function that is homogeneous of degree one in input. In addition, it is reciprocal to Farrell (1957) output-oriented measure of technical efficiency. This last observation permits decomposition of productivity change into two parts, one measuring changes in technical efficiency and one, which captures the shift in the production frontier. To define a Malmquist index requires definition of distance functions with respect to two different time's periods such as

$$D_0^t\left(x^{t+1}, y^{t+1}\right)=\inf\left\{\theta:\left(x^{t+1}, y^{t+1}/\theta\right)\in S^t\right\} \qquad ...(2a)$$

$$D_0^{t+1}\left(x^1, y^t\right)=\inf\left\{\theta:\left(x^1, y^t/\theta\right)\in S^{t+1}\right\} \qquad ...(2b)$$

The first distance function, in (2a), measures the maximum proportional changes in outputs required to make (x^{t+1}, y^{t+1}) feasible in relation to the technology at the previous period t. Similarly, the second mixed-period distance function, in (2b), measures the maximum proportional change in output required to make (x^t, y^t) feasible in relation to the technology at $(t+1)$, which we call D_0^{t+1} (x^t, y^t). In both these mixed-period cases, the value of the distance function may exceed unity. This can occur if the observation being evaluated is not feasible in the other period.

Caves, Christensen and Diewert (1982a) define an output-based Malmquist productivity index relative to a single technology t as[7]

$$M_0^t=\frac{D_0^t\left(x^{t+1}, y^{t+1}\right)}{D_0\left(x^t, y^t\right)} \qquad ...(3a)$$

and for $(t+1)$ as

$$M_0^{t+1} = \frac{D_0^{t+1}\left(x^{t+1}, y^{t+1}\right)}{D_0^{t+1}\left(x^t, y^t\right)} \qquad \text{...(3b)}$$

Fare, Grosskopf, Lindgren and Roos (1994) employed the geometric mean of the two output-based Malmquist indexes define above to yield the following Malmquist-type measure of productivity:

$$M_0\left(x^{t+1}, y^{t+1}, x^t, y^t\right) = \left[\frac{D_0^t\left(x^{t+1}, y^{t+1}\right)}{D_0^t\left(x^t, y^t\right)} \times \frac{D_0^{t+1}\left(x^{t+1}, y^{t+1}\right)}{D_0^{t+1}\left(x^t, y^t\right)}\right]^{1/2} \qquad \text{..(4)}$$

Following Fare, Grosskopf, Lindgren and Roos (1994) an equivalent way of writing this index is

$$M_0(x^{t+1}, y^{t+1}, x^t, y^t) = \frac{D_0^{t+1}\left(x^{t+1}, y^{t+1}\right)}{D_0^t\left(x^t, y^t\right)}$$

$$\left[\frac{D_0^t\left(x^{t+1}, y^{t+1}\right)}{D_0^{t+1}\left(x^{t+1}, y^{t+1}\right)} \times \frac{D_0^t\left(x^t, y^t\right)}{D_0^{t+1}(x^1, y^t)}\right]^{1/2} \qquad \text{...(5)}$$

where the ratio outside the bracket measures the change in the output-oriented measure of Farrell technical efficiency between years t and $(t+1)$. The geometric mean of the two ratios inside the bracket captures the shift in technology between the two periods evaluated at the input level x^{t+1} and the input level realized at x^t.[8]

Thus the two terms in (5) correspond to

$$\text{Efficiency change} = \frac{D_0^{t+1}\left(x^{t+1}, y^{t+1}\right)}{D_0^t\left(x^t, y^t\right)}$$

$$\text{Technical change} = \left[\frac{D_0^t\left(x^{t+1}, y^{t+1}\right)}{D_0^{t+1}\left(x^{t+1}, y^{t+1}\right)} \times \frac{D_0^t\left(x^t, y^t\right)}{D_0^{t+1}(x^t, y^t)}\right]^{1/2}$$

The efficiency change term is equivalent to the ratio of Farrell technical efficiency in period $(t+1)$ divided by Farrell technical efficiency in period *t*. The technical change term is the geometric mean of the shift in technology as observed at x^{t+1} (the first ratio inside the bracket) and the shift in technology observed at x^t (the second ratio inside the bracket).

Table 1 shows the decomposition result. The result shows that during both the eighties and nineties output growth comes increasingly from input growth. During the eighties technical efficiency was negative for four districts and ranged between 0.15 per cent (Murshidabad) to 4.01 per cent (Jalpaiguri), and the situation improved during the nineties. In this decade technical efficiency becomes negative only in two districts (Bankura and Birbhum) out of fifteen districts. On the other hand, during the eighties technology change was negative for thirteen districts out of fifteen districts and ranged between 1.12 per cent (Purulia) to 12.32 per cent (Howrah), but the situation worsened during the nineties when technology change becomes negative for all the districts and ranged between 0.34 per cent (Jalpaiguri) to 8.34 per cent (Howrah).

Table 1: Decomposition of Output Growth (per cent)

Districts	*1980-1989*			*1990-2000*			*1980-2000*		
	Output growth due to			*Output growth due to*			*Output growth due to*		
	I.G.	E.C.	T.C.	I.G.	E.C.	T.C.	I.G.	E.C.	T.C.
Midnapore	99.15	4.01	-3.16	110.23	-4.13	-6.09	103.59	0.54	-4.14
Bankura	103.36	-1.62	-1.74	106.89	-1.50	-5.38	104.56	-1.48	-3.08
Purulia	92.59	8.52	-1.12	107.94	-8.07	0.13	99.29	1.27	-0.57
Birbhum	105.28	-0.25	-5.02	103.31	-0.96	-2.35	104.23	-0.51	-3.71
Burdwan	104.43	1.26	-5.68	106.16	0.68	-6.84	104.87	0.96	-5.83
Howrah	111.37	0.94	-12.32	97.75	5.79	-3.55	105.59	2.75	-8.34
Hooghly	105.18	0.77	-5.96	103.67	2.36	-6.03	104.32	1.34	-5.67
24-Parganas	102.54	3.86	-6.40	102.85	-4.32	1.46	102.67	0.39	-3.06
Murshidabad	110.31	-0.17	-10.14	98.89	0.65	0.44	105.44	0.16	-5.60
Nadia	108.68	0	-8.68	99.79	0	0.20	104.85	0	-4.85
Malda	102.68	4.23	-6.92	100.31	-3.05	2.74	101.78	1.10	-2.89
W. Dinajpur	103.32	7.32	-10.64	107.29	-2.54	-4.74	104.86	2.97	-7.82
Coochbehar	99.58	0	0.42	104.36	0	-4.36	101.49	0	-1.49
Darjeeling	93.31	15.16	-8.47	102.92	2.80	-5.71	97.62	9.33	-6.95
Jalpaiguri	100.26	-4.01	3.74	93.49	12.44	-5.93	98.02	2.31	-0.34

I.G. = Input Growth, E.C. = Efficiency Change, T.C. = Technology Change

Technical efficiency improved slowly in all the districts throughout the period, but there was still potential to improve technical efficiency in 1990s. Thus West Bengal agriculture between 1980 and 2000 experienced low rate of technological progress together with gradual improvements in technical efficiency but output growth in the sector become increasingly depend on input growth.

The above findings have significant policy implications for promoting production growth in West Bengal agriculture. This paper supports the findings of Kumar and Rosegrant (1994), and Bhalla (1995) that increase in agricultural investments, especially in research and development, is clearly needed to stimulate technical change. Further, institutional changes should focus on achieving greater regional specialization based on comparative advantage.

Conclusion

It can be concluded from the above discussion that total factor productivity has shown dismal performance in West Bengal agriculture since the eighties. There was substantially diminished performance in the contributions of total factor productivity growth which broadly held true across districts. It is also seen that during both the period output growth come increasingly from input growth. The technical efficiency has improved during the nineties as compared to eighties but the technological progress has declined. Throughout the period, technical efficiency improved slowly, technological progress has declined and the contribution of input growth to output growth gradually increased. Thus West Bengal agriculture experienced low rate of technological progress together with gradual improvements in technical efficiency but output growth in the sector becomes increasingly dependent on input growth.

The policy implications of the foregoing analysis are as follows: (1) Technological progress and technical efficiency improvement are the two key resources of long term agricultural growth and more attention should be paid to promote them through investment in R&D and extension services; (2) The accelerated introduction of better technologies and best techniques depend on sustained investment in agricultural infrastructure including agricultural credit. The Central and State Governments' expenditures on subsidizing inputs such as power and fertilizer would be better spent on infrastructure;

and (3) Removal of subsidies should be accompanied by an efficient agricultural credit system and the National Bank for Agriculture and Rural Development should be further strengthened.

NOTES

1. A few studies (Sidhu and Byerlle, 1992; Kumar and Mruthyanjaya, 1992; Kumar and Rosegrant, 1994; Rosegrant and Evenson, 1992; Desai and Namboodiri, 1997; Pillai, 2001; Dholakia and Dholakia, 1993; etc.) in the recent years have tried to calculate Tornqvist TFPG measures or its variance. Such measures do not incorporate efficiency effects.
2. There exist wide inter-district socio-economic and agro-climatic variations in West Bengal. It enjoys seacoast, alluvial plains, extensive forest, small hillocks and red laterite plateau. Communities of different ethnic background (tribal, upper caste Hindu, lower caste people, non-Hindu groups etc.) are residing in this state.
3. The data set also provide information on district level crop prices for all these years.
4. In order to make the data comparable over years we have deflated the total value for each year in terms of a composite district (output) price index. The district price index is constructed from the district prices.
5. They treated the Malmquist index as a theoretical index. They showed that, under certain conditions, the Tornqvist index (which is readily computable) can be derived from the theoretical index.
6. See Shephard (1970) or Fare (1986) for details concerning axioms on *S*t.
7. They define the index generally, so that it could compare two firms or one firm over two periods. For the moment, we assume we are looking at one firm over two periods.
8. More precisely, the shift in the frontier is evaluated at the two different observed input levels, holding the mix of observed outputs constant as well. Since these are output distance functions the level of outputs is not held constant, but rather is expanded radically as much as is feasible given technology.

REFERENCES

1. Aigner, Lovell and Schmidt (1977), "Formulation and Estimation of Frontier Production Models", *Journal of Econometrics*, 6(4), (July).
2. Banerjee A.V., P.J. Gertler and M. Ghatak (2002), Empowerment and Efficiency: Tenancy Reform in West Bengal, *Journal of Political Economy*, 110(2).
3. Bhalla, G.S. (1995), "Globalization and Agricultural Policy in India", *Indian Journal of Agricultural Economics*, 50(1), pp. 8-26.

4. Bhalla, G.S. and G. Singh. (1997), "Recent Developments in Indian Agriculture: A State level analysis", *Economic and Political Weekly*.
5. Boyce, J.K. (1987), *Agrarian Impasse in Bengal: Institutional Constraints to Technological Change*, Oxford University Press, Oxford.
6. Caves, D.W., L.R. Christensen and E. Diewert, (1982a), "Multilateral Comparison of Output, Input and Productivity using Superlative Index Numbers", *Economic Journal*, 92.
7. Chattopadhyay, A.K. and P.S. Das. (2000), "Estimation of Growth Rate: A Critical Analysis with Reference to West Bengal Agriculture", *Indian Journal of Agricultural Economics*, 55 (2).
8. Chattopadhyay, M., C. Neogi, and S.K. Maity. (1993), "Growth and Instability in Crop Production in Eastern India", *Asian Economic Review*.
9. Desai, Bhupat M. and N.V. Namboodiri (1997), "Determination of Total Factor Productivity in Indian Agriculture", *Economic and Political Weekly*, 32(52).
10. Dholakia, Bakul H. and Ravindra H. Dholakia (1993), "Growth of Total Factor Productivity in Indian Agriculture", *Indian Economic Review*.
11. Dyer, G. (1998), "Farm size and productivity: A new look at the old debate revisited", *Economic and Political Weekly*, 33(26).
12. Fan, S. (1991), "Effects of Technological Change and Institutional Reform on Production Growth in Chinese Agriculture", *American Journal of Agricultural Economics*, 73(2), pp. 266-275.
13. Farrell, M.J., (1957), "The Measurement of Productive Efficiency", *Journal of the Royal Statistical Society*, Series A, 120(3).
14. Fare, R., (1986), "Addition and Efficiency", *Quarterly Journal of Economics*, Vol. 100.
15. Fare, R., S. Grosskopf, B. Lindgren and P. Roos (1994), "Productivity Changes in Swedish Hospitals: A Malmquist Output Index Approach", in A. Charnes, W.W. Cooper, A.Y. Lewin and L.R. Seiford (eds.), *Data Envelopment Analysis: Theory, Methodology and Application.*, Kluwer Academic Press, Boston/Dordrecht/London.
16. Kalirajan, K.P. and R.T. Shand (1997), "Sources of Output Growth in Indian Agriculture", *Indian Journal of Agricultural Economics*, Vol. 52, No. 4, October-December, pp. 693-706.
17. Kumar, P. and Mruthynjaya (1992), "Measurement and Analysis of Total Factor Productivity Growth in Wheat", *Indian Journal of Agricultural Economics*, 47(3).
18. Kumar, P. and Rosegrant Mark, W. (1994), "Productivity and Sources of Growth for Rice in India", *Economic and Political Weekly*, 19(53).
19. Malmquist, S. (1953), "Index Numbers and Indifference Surfaces", *Trabajos de Estatistica*, Vol. 4, pp. 209-242.
20. Meeusen, W. and J. van den Broeck (1977), "Efficiency Estimation from Cobb-Douglas Production Functions with Composed Error", *International Economic Review*, 18(2), pp.435-444.
21. Mukherjee, B. and S. Mukhopadhyay (1996), "Impact of Institutional Change in Productivity in a Small-Farm Economy: The Case of Rural West Bengal", in A. Raychaudhuri and D. Sarkar (Eds.) (1996), *Economy*

of West Bengal: Problems and Prospects, Allied Publishers Pvt. Ltd., New Delhi.

22. Mukhopadhyay, D. and N. Sarkar (2001), "Has There Been an Acceleration in the Growth of Agriculture in West Bengal: A Fresh Look Using Modern Time Series Techniques", *Sankhya Series B*, 63 (1).
23. Nishmizu, M. and J.M. Page (1982), "Total Factor Productivity Growth, Technological Progress and Technical Efficiency Change: Dimensions of Productivity Change in Yugoslavia 1965-78", *Economic Journal, 92.*
24. Pillai, Renuka (2001), "An Analysis of Paddy Productivity Growth in West Bengal and Orissa", *Indian Journal of Agricultural Economics.*
25. Rawal, V. and M. Swaminathan. (1998), "Changing Trajectories: Agricultural Growth in West Bengal, 1950 to 1996", *Economic and Political Weekly,* 33(40), pp.2595-2602.
26. Raychaudhuri, A. and A.K. Sen (1996), "Agricultural Reform and Productivity: Some Important Lessons to be Learnt from West Bengal's Operation Barga", in A. Raychaudhuri and D. Sarkar (Eds.) (1996), *Economy of West Bengal: Problems and Prospects*, Allied Publishers Pvt. Ltd., New Delhi.
27. Rosegrant Mark W. and Robert E. Evenson (1992), Agricultural Productivity and Source of Growth in South Asia", *American Journal of Agricultural Economics*, Vol.74.
28. Rudra, A. (1992), *Political Economy of Indian Agriculture*, K.P. Bagchi and Company, Calcutta.
29. Saha, A. and M. Swaminathan. (1994), "Agricultural Growth in West Bengal in the 1980s: A Disaggregation by Districts and Crops", *Economic and Political Weekly*, 29 (13).
30. Sanyal, M.K., P.K. Biswas and S. Barahan (1998), "Institutional Change and Output Growth in West Bengal Agriculture: End and Impasse", *Economic and Political Weekly*, 33(47-48), pp.2979-2986.
31. Sawant, S.D. and C.V. Achuthan. (1995), "Agricultural Growth across Crops and Regions: Emerging Trends and Patterns", *Economic and Political Weekly.*
32. Sen, A. and S. Sengupta. (1995), "*The Recent Growth in Agricultural Output in Eastern India with Special Reference to the Case of West Bengal*", paper presented at the Workshop on 'Agricultural Growth and Agrarian Structure in Contemporary West Bengal and Bangladesh', Calcutta: Centre for Studies in Social Sciences, January 9-12.
33. Sengupta A., Bhattacharya J. and Chattopadhyay M. (2004), "Agricultural Growth and Welfare: A Study on Indian States". *South Asia Economic Journal*, 5(1).
34. Shepherd, R.W. (1970), *Theory of Cost and Production Functions*, Princeton, Princeton University Press.
35. Sidhu, D.S. and D. Byerlee (1991), "Technical Change and Wheat Productivity in Post-Green Revolution Punjab", *Economic and Political Weekly*, 26(52), pp. A159-A166.

10

Privatization of Life Insurance Sector: Analyzing the Pros and Cons

Joy Chakraborty

Introduction

From a single government insurer (L.I.C.I.) till the mid-nineties, the Indian insurance industry post-privatization underwent a drastic change that witnessed the market share of private insurance players to soar up to 25.61 per cent at the end of the financial year 2007-08. The Life Insurance Corporation of India (L.I.C.I.) dominated the life insurance market in India with its age-old conventional products and a large customer-base. In the nineties, the scenario changed following the introduction of reform measures by the Government in the area of life insurance in an attempt to infuse more fresh capital in the insurance arena. In the post-reform era, the insurance sector in India underwent a sea change with more and more private participants pouring in. With their entry, the private players have also brought in highly customized products and aggressive marketing strategies thereby infusing more professionalism into the sector.

Though the existing insurance law allowed a foreign partner to hold 26 per cent equity in an insurance company in India, a proposal to augment this limit from 26 per cent to 49 per cent was pending with the government. Had the proposed law came to fruition, it would have enabled the foreign companies to infuse fresh capital in the Indian insurance sector, thereby fuelling further growth. Apart from this issue, the private life insurance players confronted numerous challenges in selling their products and attracting investments.

The paper proceeds as follows: Section1 provides an overview of the Indian life insurance sector. Section 2 provides an overview of the growth prospects and challenges of the Indian Life Insurance sector. Finally, Section 3 provides the changing scenario of the Indian life Insurance sector along with the concluding observations.

Section 1: Indian Life Insurance Sector: An Industry Overview

From time immemorial human beings had always been in search of security. The story of evolution of mankind was in fact a saga of continuous pursuit of a secured life. This urge for protection led to the concept of insurance. The Greeks and the Romans were the first to introduce health and life insurance in 600 A.D. through the establishment of guilds entitled as "benevolent societies" which looked after the families and paid funeral expenses to members upon death. In the modern society the evolution of insurance business started off with the marine business in England during the late 1680s under the initiative of Mr. Edward Lloyd.

The Insurance laws in India were developed in the footsteps of English Insurance Laws. The insurance business in India started off with the marine business as was the case in England and gradually extended to other businesses like life and fire. At that time, the policies were sold to the businessmen of Indian origin in excess of the normal prevalent rates based on the assumption that the expected life of Indians was less and more risk-prone. In 1871, the first Indian company named "Bombay Mercantile Life Assurance Society" commenced its business operations in India at normal rates of premium, i.e. at the rate applicable to the English people. This was followed by the establishment of "The Oriental Government Security Life Assurance Company" in 1874, the "Bharat" in 1896 and the "Empire of India" in 1897. These and several other Indian companies were started as a result of the Swadeshi Movement in the early 1900s. At this stage, in order to check the mushrooming of the life insurance business and its agencies, the need for a regulating authority was recognized for the first time that took shape in the form of the "Indian LIC Act" in 1912.

The period between 1928 and 1956 held a significant aspect in the development of insurance laws in India. During this period, a serious attention was paid to modify the insurance laws to infuse professionalism in the Indian insurance sector with the introduction of innovative products and an attempt was made to educate the masses about the benefits of insurance. As a result, a new Insurance Act was adopted in 1938 to monitor the activities of life insurance companies in India. The enactment of the Insurance Act, 1938 provided stability to the growing insurance business and the earlier legislations were consolidated and amended to protect the interest of the insuring public. The next significant piece of legislation that came into effect was the introduction of the Life Insurance Act on September 1, 1956. The nationalization of the life insurance business in India saw the emergence of country's only public-sector life insurance company, Life Insurance Corporation of India (L.I.C.I.), which was formed as a result of the takeover of 170 companies and 75 provident fund societies. This initiated the rising dominance of L.I.C.I. in the Indian insurance sector that prevailed till the 1990s, when the Government of India proposed reforms in the insurance sector to end the monopoly and dominance of the public sector life insurance company in India.

Prompted by the impact of liberalization and globalization of the Indian economy in the early 1990s, the Government of India appointed a high-powered committee entitled "Malhotra Committee" in 1993 under the chairmanship of R.N. Malhotra, former Finance Secretary and Governor of Reserve Bank of India (RBI). The Malhotra Committee, formed by the Government. of India, was entrusted to examine and propose measures to reform the Indian insurance sector. The committee submitted its report in January 1994 that recommended the establishment of strong and effective insurance regulatory authority in the form of statutory body. Among the recommendations, capital investment for life and general insurance business in India was increased to Rs. 100 crores. The committee predominantly emphasized upon the private-sector participation in the life insurance business thereby lifting the entry barriers of private players and allowing foreign players to enter the market with some limits (26%) on foreign direct investment. On the basis of the Malhotra Committee recommendations, the Central Government enacted the Insurance Regulatory and Development Authority (IRDA) Act in 1999. The formation of this act opened the floodgates of opportunities for the private players in India to diversify themselves into the insurance business either through joint ventures or as a standalone player. Following the opening up of the insurance sector, four new insurance companies (Birla Sun life Insurance Company, ICICI Prudential Life Insurance Company, Max New York Life Insurance Company, and HDFC Standard Life Insurance Company Ltd.) commenced their operations in 2000-2001.

Section 2: Private Life Insurers: Scaling Pinnacles of Excellence

At the beginning of 2008, there were 18 registered life insurance companies in India with one public-sector player and 17 private insurers. With the retail giant Pantaloons and IDBI Bank coming into the picture, the number of private life insurers operating in India has risen to 17, with more proposals being on the pipeline. At the end of the financial year 2007-08, there were 21 registered life insurance companies that were operating in India with 1 public-sector player and 20 private insurers (Table1), with more proposals being on the pipeline. The above data itself manifested a rise in the number of private players from 15 to 20 within a span of just 1 year.

Table 1: Life Insurance Companies operating in India during 2007-08

Public Sector	*Private Players*
1. Life Insurance Corpora-tion of India (LIC)	1. Bajaj Allianz Life Insurance Co. Ltd
	2. Birla Sun Life Insurance Co. Ltd. (BSLI)
	3. HDFC Standard Life Insurance Co. Ltd. (HDFC STD LIFE)
	4. ICICI Prudential Life Insurance Co. Ltd. (ICICI PRU)
	5. IG Vysya Ufe Insurance Co. Ltd.(ING VYSYA)
	6. Max NEW YORK Life Insurance Co. Ltd. (MNYL)
	7. MetLife India Insurance Co Pvt. Ltd. (METLIFE)
	8. Kotak Mahindra Old Mutual Life Insurance Co. Ltd.
	9. SBI Life Insurance Co. Ltd (SBI LIFE)
	10. TATAAIG Life Insurance Co. Ltd. (TATAAIG)
	11. Reliance Life Insurance Company Ltd.
	12. Aviva Life Insurance Co. Pvt. Ltd.(AVIVA)
	13. Sahara India Life Insurance Go. Ltd. (SAHARA LIFE)
	14. Shriram Life Insurance Co. Ltd. (SHRIRAM LIFE)
	15. Bharti AXA Life Insurance Co. Ltd. (BHARTI AXA)
	16. Future General India Life Insurance Co. Ltd. (FUTURE GENERAL INDIA LIFE)
	17. IDBI Fortis Life Insurance Co. Ltd.
	18. Canara HSBC Oriental Bank of Commerce Life Insurance Co. Ltd
	19. Aegon Religare Life Insurance Company Limited.
	20. DLF Pranerica Life Insurance Co. Ltd.

Source: Compiled by the authors from IRDA website and IRDA Annual Reports

L.I.C.I. was the standalone player in the Indian insurance market before the entry of private insurance players. Since the liberalization of the insurance sector in 1999, the market share of private life insurance players had increased by leaps and bounds. This was largely because of the introduction of innovative products, smart insurance marketing and aggressive selling and distribution strategies that enabled the private players to augment its customer-base faster than expected. Table 2 provides the details.

Table 2: L.I.C.I. vs. Leading Private Insurer in terms of Product Variation

Life Insurance Products	*L.I.C.I.*	*ICICI Prudential*
Term Insurance Policy	Yes	Yes
Whole Life Policy	Yes	Yes
Endowment Policy	Yes	Yes
Money Back Policy	Yes	Yes
Annuities and Pensions	Yes	Yes
Critical illness Policies	No	Yes
Education Insurance Policies	Yes	Yes
Wealth Creation Policies	No	Yes
Unit Linked Products	Yes	Yes
Senior Citizen Policies	Yes	No
Micro-insurance Policies	Yes	No

Source: Compiled by the Author.

The new policies issued by the industry amounted to 35.4 million during 2005-06, compared to 26.2 million sold during the previous year. While the private life insurers exhibited a dynamic growth of 73.4 per cent in selling the new policies, L.I.C.I. reported a mere growth of 31.8 per cent. The private insurance players even garnered a 122.6 per cent growth in 2005-06 in total renewal premium income as compared to 14.3 per cent growth of L.I.C.I. in 2004-05. During the five-year period, i.e. from 2003-04 to 2007-08, the Life insurance companies sold a total of 187325954 policies. Out of these, L.I.C.I. sold 158378790 policies (85% of the total). The remaining 15 per cent went to the private Life Insurers. In 2004-05, the life insurance companies sold a total of 26211198 new policies. Of this, L.I.C.I. sold 23978123 policies (market share: 91.48%) while the private sector life insurers sold 2233075 new policies (market share: 8.52%). This again reflected a sharp rise in the market share of private life insurers from 8.52 per cent in 2004-05 to 15 per cent at the end of 2007-08. Table 3 provides the details. This reflected the amazing persistency of the private life insurance companies in keeping up with the challenges of L.I.C.I.

With a large population and untapped market, life insurance companies were a major instrument for mobilizing the savings of people and ranked next to the banking institutions in India.

Table 3: No. of New Policies Sold by Life Insurance Companies (2003-04 to 2007-08)

Insurer	*2003-04*	*2004-05*	*2005-06*	*2006-07*	*2007-08*
LIC	26968069	23978123	31590707	38229292	37612599
Private Life Insurers	1658847	2233075	3871410	7922274	13261558
Total	28626916	26211198	35462117	46151566	50874157

Source: IRDA (2006): Fifth Annual Report (2004-05), www.irdaindia.org

In spite of that, insurance penetration levels remained at a low level of 24 per cent in 2006 thereby exhibiting the hugely untapped potential of the life insurance market in India. Insurance penetration for the year 2005 stood at 2.53 per cent for life insurance which was well below the global average of 4.34 per cent of the Gross Domestic Product (GDP). Table 4 provides the details.

Table 4: Life Insurance Penetration Levels: International Comparison

Country/Region	*2003*	*2004*	*2005*	*2006*	*2007*
India	2.26	2.53	2.53	4.10	4.00
Asia	4.82	5.58	5.16	5.00	4.60
World	4.59	4.55	4.34	4.50	4.40

Note: Insurance penetration is measured as ratio (in %) of premium to GDP

Source: I.R.D.A. Annual Reports.

Saturation of markets in many developed economies has made the Indian market even more attractive for global insurance majors. In addition, the private players had a second-mover advantage over its predecessor L.I.C.I. in fruitfully strategizing its business options. The private players garnered valuable lessons from the mistakes and achievements of L.I.C.I. and accordingly mitigated its own risks and investment requirements. Further, the adoption of new and innovative technologies by the private players was found to enhance their performances compared to L.I.C.I. who remained engrossed in applying traditional business methodologies. Several private life insurers such as Tata-AIG Life and Max New York Life have developed a renewal premium collection team to make the policyholders aware about their probable premium dates and payment options. In a bid to tap the rural insurable population, Bajaj Allianz has started to establish several sales service offices throughout India, almost in the similar lines of L.I.C.I., mostly in the neighbourhoods of major cities. Barring L.I.C.I., the top five private life insurers has adopted aggressive bancassurance strategies, through the tie-up with several nationalized and private banks in India, to promote their products. Even the private life insurers have set-up call centres and introduced on-line payment of premiums to facilitate the customers respectively with their queries and smart payment options. In addition, private life insurers such as ICICI Prudential have come up with aggressive marketing and advertising strategies that imprinted an indelible impression on the minds of the customers. In addition to the conventional perception of an insurance product, the company has also positioned its policies as investment products. It's "CHINTAMANI" series of advertisements continuously emphasized on the importance of insurance policies as a wealth maximization tool. ICICI Prudential represented "CHINTAMANI" as the mascot of the middle class which later on gained popularity among the masses.

Thanks to him, ICICI Prudential increased its insurance brand recall to 92 per cent, next to L.I.C.I.'s 97 per cent in 2005. However, the global insurance giants had to initially sail through the uncharted waters before strengthening their foothold in India. Given the high establishment and initial operating expenses, it became difficult for the insurers to earn profits in the initial five to seven years of their operations. Initial operating costs of an Insurance company related to cost rate of commissions payable in the first year, expenses towards setting up operations, training costs incurred towards developing the agency force, creating a niche for its products, achieving reasonable levels of persistency, providing for policy liabilities, and maintaining the solvency margin. Thanks to its banking operations that conducted its insurance activities through a wide distribution network of 14000 branches, SBI Life Insurance Company became the first private sector company to turnaround with a net profit of Rs. 2.03 crore in 2005-06.

Apart from the cost-factor, the private life insurance companies also confronted stiff challenges from the country's only public-sector life insurance company in respect of selling insurance products. The major challenges had evolved from L.I.C.I. who had an astronomical customer-base besides enjoying the confidence and trust of the huge Indian population. On account of traditional orthodox thoughts and beliefs, most people in India preferred government organizations like L.I.C.I. Past scams along with the bankruptcy of a few private companies had further triggered the lack of trust in private insurers. The other major impediment had been the lack of knowledge about insurance benefits. People generally viewed insurance as a tax-saving device and were found to be ignorant about the insurance benefits. They never imagined that they require safeguarding their dependants in case of untimely death or from any other unforeseen contingencies.

Customer-services had been the prime focus area of the private insurance players. They tried to capitalize on the fact that people's necessities revolved around highly customized products and services that were delivered at a faster pace. Again with the rise in the number of insurance companies in India, there had been considerable increase in their telemarketing activities trying to educate and market their products to the prospective customers. The efforts of telemarketing executives, often at odd hours and on holidays irritated and created confusion among the people. Due to this, people averted in taking such calls. Even when marketing executives from several insurance companies physically approached the customers with insurance products in their offices or at home, the consumer response was also found to be unfavourable most of the time owing to the rigorous amount of work-pressure and insecurity that the common people had to bear in their everyday lives. Life Insurance companies faced several other problems owing to the distribution channels they resorted to while selling their insurance products. To break the distribution barriers, these companies tied-up with banks, corporate agents, channel partners and broking firms to market their products to the customers. Table 5 provides the details.

However, these distribution channels often proved to be ineffective owing to lack of infrastructural and delivery facilities. The insurance companies were primarily concentrated in urban and developed areas of the country. As a result, the semi-urban and rural regions of the country remained untouched and neglected. Lack of infrastructure, long-distance from cities, poor distribution and involvement of high expenditure deterred the private insurance companies to explore the business opportunities in the rural areas. Insurance agents, who were considered to be the fulcrum of the insurance business, usually came from poverty-afflicted families

Table 5: New business (life) underwritten through various intermediaries: 2007-08 (in %)

Life Insurer	*Individual Agents*	*Corporate Agents*		*Brokers*	*Direct Selling*	*Total*	*Referrals*
		Banks	*Others**				
Private Total	59.81	18.89	11.03	1.50	8.78	100.00	7.79
LC#	98.36	1.30	0.29	0.05	–	100.00	–
Industry Total	83.75	7.97	4.36	0.60	3.33	100.00	2.95

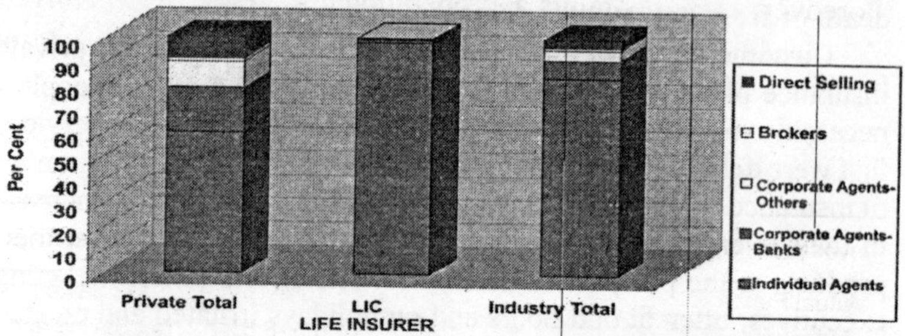

#Does note include its overseas new business premium.

Notes: (1) New business premium includes first year premium and single premium.

(2) The leads obtained through referral arrangements have been included in the respective channels.

with little or no elementary education. They, therefore, lacked etiquettes and proper mannerisms required for selling insurance products. They were also found to be unreceptive to training programmes conducted in order to upgrade their knowledge and skills. Moreover, with the entry of private players it was found that the insurance agents served numerous insurance companies at a time and misleaded the public with false assurances of high monetary gains. This lacked the motivational and commitment aspect of the agents to any particular life insurance company. As the Indian insurance market became more and more competitive owing to the entry of private players, the sales managers forced the agents to meet the targets and vie for the numbers-game. As a result the agents sold the products as per the directions of the manager rather than selling the policies as per the client's requirements. This, push-sales instead of need-based sales strategy, adopted by the private insurance players resulted in low customer satisfaction thereby affecting their performance. In addition, Life Insurance products faced stiff competition from other options which provided similar benefits like Government Bonds (fixed growth, safety), Fixed Deposits (safety, liquidity), Mutual Funds (growth, liquidity and tax benefits), NSC (safety, liquidity and tax benefits), Post Office Savings (safety, growth, liquidity) etc. Many people believed that life insurance companies had a longer lock-in investment period than any other forms of investment thereby completely ignoring the security aspect associated with a life insurance policy. Table 6 provides the details. Moreover, entry restraints and operational trade barriers involved with the functioning of a private life insurance company in India further aggravated the situation.

Table 6: A Comparison among the Various Investment Options available in India

Investment Options	*Lock-in period (in Years)*	*Return (%)*	*Added Benefits*
Mutual Funds	3	10%-15%	Tax Saving
Life Insurance	15	6.5 -8.5%	Tax Saving and Life cover
National Savings Certificate	6	8.00%	Tax Saving
Monthly Income Scheme	6	8.00%	Recurring
Fixed Deposits	1.5 - 5	8% - 10%	Tax Saving
Fixed Deposits (tax saving)	5	8.00%	Tax Saving
Provident Fund (P.F.)	15	8.00%	Tax Saving
Reserve Bank Bonds	Withdrawn		
Kishan Vikas Patra	8.5	8.00%	

Source: Compiled by the Author.

Section 3: Concluding Observations

The Indian insurance sector was at a nascent stage with plenty of growth opportunities for the private insurers to capitalize on. A survey conducted by the Max New York-NCAER India Financial Protection pointed out that in spite of the awareness about life insurance among Indians, close to 78 per cent, the penetration levels remained unimpressive. Majority of the people viewed insurance as a tax-saving device and risk coverage became a secondary objective. The survey even indicated that more than half of the population (51%) preferred to keep their surplus funds in bank deposits while 36 per cent of the population was comfortable in keeping their deposits at home. Only a miniscule 2 per cent of the

Indian population invested their savings in buying life insurance policies. The study even found that urban households (38%) held more life insurance products than rural households (19%). In a bid to tap the rural markets in India, the private insurers emphasized on selling need-based products rather than push-sales. Customers generally considered several aspects such as price, service of the company, maturity benefits and total protection before finally going for the product. As a result, private insurers were trying hard to launch several innovative products and services in an effort to increase consumer interests and awareness about the benefits of insurance. The competition had also increased among the private players in order to grab a significant market share. In a bid to spread consumer awareness, the private insurance companies has resorted to varied marketing strategies such as online marketing or e-marketing, opening up of make-shift sales outlets in different rural and semi-urban regions of the country, tie-ups with Regional Rural Banks (RRBs) for selling micro-insurance products, tie-ups with hospitals for selling health insurance products, tie-ups with retail outlets such as Pantaloons and Big Bazaar and offering insurance products based on the amount of purchases made by the customers. To further fuel growth in the insurance sector, the Government of India was in the process of introducing a "Comprehensive Insurance Amendment Bill" that would hike the investment limit of foreign players from 26 per cent to 49 per cent. With the FDI hike, the foreign insurers would be interested to infuse fresh capital in the country's insurance market. Moreover, this would increase the presence of foreign investors in the Indian insurance market. With the entry of new private players in the Indian insurance arena, there would be ample opportunities of business-growth with the industry turning out to be highly competitive. Analysts opined that with the growing number of foreign players, the state player L.I.C.I.'s market share would dip to around 50 per cent over a span of 15 years or more. With impressive technological progress offered by these private players, there would soon be a situation when customers would be able to transfer insurance payments through any ATM terminal anywhere in the country. Few private players were also tinkering with the issue of improving its services to key clients by appointing key account managers for the job who would also be responsible in augmenting the client-base of the respective insurance companies.

The Government of India and IRDA came out with numerous reform initiatives to amend the insurance laws for the benefit of the society at large. The Indian Union Budget (2007-08) emphasized upon the development of the country's insurance sector with deductions in medical insurance Under Section 80D being raised to Rs. 15,000 and Rs. 20,000 for general and senior citizens respectively. The Department of Economic Affairs (DEA) proposed to correct the existing provisions of the existing Insurance Act to enforce the life insurers to abide by the insurance contract and honour a policy at the time of settling the claim. At the time of materialization of such claims, the validity of a policy won't be questioned even on the ground that wrong statements were voluntarily produced at the time of filling up the insurance proposal form. The move, aimed at protecting consumer's interest, would assume significance in the light of large-scale participation in the life insurance business. The Indian Government and IRDA jointly monitored the sea-change developments that have been taking place in the country's insurance sector. The IRDA had a cautious look on the life insurance companies that were claiming to offer astronomical returns on their products. Even a Bombay High Court ruling allowed the trading of life insurance policies. This was a major step taken by the Government to curb the number of discontinued policies and make the system flawless.

However, there was no denying the fact that the Indian insurance sector was poised to achieve new heights in the upcoming years. Even the Associated Chambers of Commerce and Industry of India (ASSOCHAM) had reported that the Indian insurance industry, from its existing value of Rs. 2292 billion. Table 7 provides the details.

Critics opined that a large segment of rural and semi-urban area was still untouched because of long distances and poor distribution facilities. It was high time that the private life insurers capitalized on this fact and started penetrating more into the hinterland regions of the country. This was because more semi-urban and rural populace was expected to opt for insurance cover for a secure future. It thus remained a debatable point whether the private life insurers would be capable enough to tap the unexplored areas of the country faster than L.I.C.I. It also remained to be seen too what extent privatization of the life insurance sector helps to tap the unexposed insurance market of a developing country, like India.

Table 7: Key Market Indicators (2007-08)

Life and non-life market in india	Rs. 2,29,175 crore
(Total Premium)	US Dollar 54.375 billion*
Global insurance market	US Dollar 4061 billion
Inflation adjusted growth in total premium in India:	13.0 per cent (35.0 per cent in 2006-07)
Growth in premium (world) underwritten 2007-08	Life: 5.4 per cent Non-life: 0.7 per cent
Geographical restriction for new players	None
Equity restriction	Foreign promoter can hold up to 26 per cent of the equity
Registration restriction	Composite registration not available

Source: Compiled by the authors from IRDA website and IRDA Annual Reports.

REFERENCES

1. Boles James, Brashear Thomas, Bellenger Danny and Barksdale Jr. Hiram (2000), "Relationship selling behaviours: antecedents and relationship with performance", *Journal of Business and Industrial Marketing*, MCB University Press, Vol.15, No. 2/3, pp. 141-153.
2. Rice Eamonn (2001), "The Future of the Insurance Market— Do Insurers Need Crystal Balls?", MCB University Press, pp. 14-16.
3. Mathew Joseph, Stone George and Anderson Krista (2003), "Insurance customers' assessment of service quality: a critical evaluation", *Journal of Small Business and Enterprise Development*, MCB UP Limited, Volume 10, Number 1, pp. 81-92.
4. Chakraborty, J. (2007): "Private Life Insurance Companies in India: Growing Prospects and Challenges", *Insurance Chronicle Magazine on Risk Management*, pp. 29-39, ICFAI University Press.
5. —— (2008): "Private Life Insurance Companies in India: Strategizing Ways to Overcome the Product-Selling Challenges", *Journal of Risk and Insurance*, pp.7-20, ICFAI University Press.
6. IRDA: Annual Reports, 2003-04, 2004-05, 2005-06, 2006-07, 2007-08, www.irdaindia.org
7. R. Powers Michael (2006), "Insurance Paradox", *The Journal of Risk Finance*, Emerald Group Publishing Limited, Vol. 7, No. 2, pp. 113-116.
8. Menon Radhika, "When insurers make their pitch", *Hindu Business Line,* April 21,2005, http://www.thehindubusinessline.com/catalyst/2005/04/21/stories/2005042100080100.htm

9. Boulding William and Christen Markus, "First-Mover Disadvantage", http://ged.insead.fr/fichiersti/inseadwp 2001/2001-03.pdf
10. "GoM to meet on insurance FDI", *Times Business News*, Kolkata, March 20, 2007.

Index